6.95

# Follow Up French

# Related titles in the series

# Follow Up French

## *Made Simple*

John Roper

*Formerly Head of Languages,
Shenfield School, Essex*

**MADE SIMPLE
BOOKS**

Made Simple
An imprint of Butterworth-Heinemann Ltd
Linacre House, Jordan Hill, Oxford OX2 8DP

 PART OF REED INTERNATIONAL BOOKS

OXFORD  LONDON  BOSTON
MUNICH  NEW DELHI  SINGAPORE  SYDNEY
TOKYO  TORONTO  WELLINGTON

First published 1992

**British Library Cataloguing in Publication Data**
A catalogue record for this book is available
from the British Library

ISBN 0 7506 0236 8

Typeset by Keygraphics, Aldermaston, Berkshire
Printed in England by Clays Ltd, St Ives plc

15|12|92

# Contents

# Preface

*Follow up French* gives:

- practical advice on ways to improve the language skills of listening, reading, speaking and writing
- a concise guide to understanding French grammar
- examples of methods of testing, exercises and extracts of post GCSE examinations (with answers in Part 6)
- details of examinations available and a bibliography of useful addresses
- information on how to use French for work or pleasure

The book can be supplemented by an audio tape which contains much useful recorded material for listening and speaking.

*Follow up French* may be used on its own or in conjunction with other courses. Post GCSE students, whether studying privately, in the sixth form, at a College of Further Education or at an Adult Education Centre, will find it an invaluable aid to their studies.

# Acknowledgements

I would like to thank the following Examination Boards for permission to use some of their past papers as examples of post GCSE examinations:

    Associated Examining Board
    Joint Matriculation Board Examinations Council
    University of London School Examinations Board
    University of Oxford Delegacy of Local Examinations
    Institute of Linguists
    London Chamber of Commerce and Industry Examinations Board
    RSA Examinations Board

In addition I am grateful to the following for allowing me to use material to illustrate certain sections of the book:

*L'Express* for permission to use the article 'L'Europe fait peau neuve'. Editions Gallimard for permission to print the poem 'Les Lilas et les Roses' (Crève-Coeur) by Louis Aragon, and the extract from *Vol de Nuit* by Antoine de Saint-Exupéry.
Eurotunnel for permission to quote from their publicity material.

My thanks are due also to Ms Jacquie Shanahan, the Commissioning Editor, for her help and advice, Nicole Tosser for her useful comments, and particularly to my wife Barbara who not only typed the MS (in itself not an easy task) but whose common-sense criticisms helped to shape the whole book.

*J.R.*

# Part One
## Improving Language Skills

Language acquisition can be broken down into four skill areas – reading, listening, speaking and writing. It is important not to treat each one as a separate, unrelated skill. All are inter-related and supportive. Reading French will help you when you come to write it; listening to French will help you to speak it better. In this book the four skills are treated separately but each section will help you improve your overall performance in the language. You will be told how to improve your skill in each area, shown how they are tested, be given sample questions and model answers. Two other important areas of study in post GCSE language learning are those of literature and 'civilization', i.e. background knowledge in depth of the culture, customs, traditions, political systems of France and general information concerning the country and its people. Students are asked to write about these in English or French, sometimes under examination conditions, sometimes as a piece of more elaborate research. Advice will be given on how to tackle these aspects of further language study.

# 1
# Speaking

The claim that the English make poor linguists is untrue. There is no reason why English people should not speak French just as well as the Dutch, for example, master English. The fact that English is an international lingua franca did, until recently, militate against the pressing need to learn a foreign language, but it is now universally recognized that to compete on equal terms in foreign markets you must be able to speak the language of the country in which you are conducting business.

Speaking is an active skill and best practised with a partner or in company with other French speakers, so try to find some person, or persons, with whom you can converse on a regular basis. Local native speakers, assistants, evening classes, French circles are all sources to tap.

Listening is a complementary skill and the material recorded on the tape for this section of the book will help your spoken French by increasing your vocabulary and giving you models to imitate.

## Techniques for improvement of spoken French

Many students are hesitant to speak French for fear of sounding odd and/or making grammatical mistakes. Don't allow either of these barriers to stop you from attempting to express yourself in French. Many people find English spoken with a French accent attractive. The same applies in reverse and, although you should make every endeavour to speak as naturally as possible, do not think that a poor accent is always the subject of ridicule. How often in everyday speech do we express ourselves in complete, grammatically perfect sentences? Rarely. Do not expect therefore, your French sentences to be examples of perfectly formed, error-free language. Learn to live with errors. The most important thing is to open your mouth and start talking.

Spoken language is not the same as written language. When speaking, we express our thoughts in incomplete sentences, we use circumlocutions when the right word eludes us, we repeat phrases, we run words together and omit others. The spoken language is fleeting and ephemeral. Unless it is being recorded for a particular purpose, it will not be analysed for discussion and correction at a later date. Its task is immediate and if you make false starts, are hesitant, repeat yourself, make mistakes (providing that these do not alter the sense of what you want to say) you can still succeed in your main aim which is to get your message across.

In conversation you do not have time to formulate complete sentences before uttering them. There are, however, many phrases which you can use to 'link and think', i.e. give you time to marshal your thoughts before carrying on the conversation. You may wish to expand the theme, refute the argument, express surprise, joy, dismay, etc., or conclude the conversation. Listen out for these expressions and build up your own stock.

## Link and think

| | |
|---|---|
| En effet, ce que je veux dire, c'est … | In fact, what I mean is … |
| Oui, on peut dire aussi … | Yes, you can say that too … |
| On peut ajouter … | One can add … |
| Moi aussi, je trouve que … | I, also, find that … |
| C'est à dire … | That is to say … |
| De toute façon … | In any case … |
| A part ça … | Besides that … |
| Ben oui … | Oh! yes … |
| D'accord … | Agreed … |
| O.K. | O.K. |
| Bien sûr … | Of course … |
| Tu penses …? | Do you think (so) …? |
| Vraiment? | Really? |
| Mais non! | Oh no! |
| Moi, je ne suis pas d'accord … | I don't agree … |
| De l'autre côté on peut dire … | On the other hand it can be said … |
| Il ne faut pas oublier … | You must not forget … |
| En revanche … | On the other hand/in return … |
| A mon avis … | In my opinion … |
| Comment! | What! |
| Oh là là! | Dear, dear! |
| Dis donc! | I say! |
| Pas vrai! | Not true! |
| C'est extraordinaire/bizarre … | It's extraordinary/really odd … |
| Que c'est bête! | How silly that is! |
| C'est mignon … | It's delightful … |
| Mince! | Lovely! |
| Désolé! | I'm sorry! |
| C'est ça. | That's it. |

C'est tout ce que je veux dire.     That's all I want to say.

Common expressions are often run together in one utterance, and the negative particle 'ne' is usually suppressed in speech.

> sais pas
> j'veux pas
> j'en sais rien

Questions too, are usually expressed by intonation or by using 'est-ce que' rather than the more formal inversion found in the written language.

Don't forget the dual functions of a tape recorder – to record as well as to play back. Read and record a passage of French and, if possible, compare it to the same passage spoken by a native speaker.

Set aside a cassette for recording new expressions you have come across in spoken French – a vocabulary of the spoken word. Replay it regularly to reinforce the new words. A car radio or personal stereo is ideal for this. If you don't mind talking to yourself (and providing no one is listening!) talk to your recorder instead in French. Make a diary of the day's events, describe people and places, give your comments on the news or articles or books you have read. Tell a joke, even sing a song in French, if you are so inclined.

The more you use French, the more your confidence will grow and confidence is the key to greater fluency.

## Practising speaking

The exercises recorded on the accompanying tape will help you to speak French better and are also examples of some of the tasks you are asked to perform by many examination boards. Examiners always give you time to study visual matter before asking you to comment on it.

Use the pause button on your tape to give you time to think before replying and to separate the questions.

## Role play

*(Based on a Communicative Task set by the University of Oxford Delegacy of Local Examinations: A and A/S Levels.)*

Read the instructions and extract from the English brochure and then answer the questions in French.

*Feuille du candidat*
**Situation**     Vous faites partie d'un groupe scolaire de 30 étudiants qui font une visite d'études en France. Vous êtes le seul qui parle couramment le français.

**Tâche**  Pendant votre séjour vous faites la connaissance d'un(e) étudiant(e) français(e), qui vous demande en quoi consiste le cours suivi par les divers membres du groupe. Utilisez l'extrait de la brochure anglaise pour lui donner des renseignements sur le cours. Il n'est pas nécessaire de traduire le texte – essayez plutôt d'en résumer les aspects principaux.

---

# Artists in Paris

## THE COURSE

Pupils have the opportunity of seeing the environment which inspired artists of the 19th Century whose ideas influenced major changes in the development of art.

The Course concentrates on the work of Impressionist painters who lived and worked in and around Paris, but also leads you through the main art movements of past centuries. Attention is drawn to the influence of earlier painters and the effect of Impressionist paintings on subsequent modern art.

Selected paintings in the Louvre, Musée d'Orsay, Orangerie and other galleries highlight the changing attitudes and approaches to painting and new techniques of painting introduced by the Impressionist painters. A written trail helps pupils explore the Montmartre area, highlighting points of interest. The area is still popular with artists, and pupils will see artists at work and have the opportunity to record their own impressions of the city from some of the best vantage points of Paris. There is also an opportunity to visit Giverny, the home of Monet and the inspiration of many of his works, or the Barbizon area where many Impressionist painters went to work.

---

### Interpreting information and statistics

*(Based on an A Level Oral task set by AEB.)*
Read this extract and examine the table which follows it, then answer the questions on the tape.

### Radio: la musique
### plus que l'information

L'écoute de la radio, tant en fréquence qu'en durée, augmente avec l'âge chez les jeunes.

Si les étudiants déclarent écouter la radio aussi souvent que les autres jeunes, ils l'écoutent moins longtemps en moyenne: 11 heures contre 15 heures par semaine.

Les jeunes, plus que la moyenne nationale, écoutent volontiers les radios «libres» (environ un sur trois). Les étudiants (plus d'un sur deux) déclarent écouter les radios locales, contre 30% parmi les non-étudiants.

Ils semblent écouter la radio surtout comme *un bruit de fond* plus que comme une source d'information. Ils ont une prédilection pour les émissions de variétés et de chansons (46% contre 22% pour les adultes) et s'intéressent moins qu'eux à l'information (15-24 ans: 18%; 25 ans et plus: 35%).

| Les émissions les plus écoutées sont: (en %) | Chansons | Rock, pop, folk | Grande musique |
|---|---|---|---|
| Ensemble | 38,1 | 15,0 | 13,6 |
| 15-19 ans | 43,8 | 48,4 | 4,5 |
| 20-24 ans | 41,6 | 39,9 | 6,3 |
| *Total* | *42,7* | *44,2* | *5,4* |
| 25-59 ans | 45,0 | 10,5 | 18,0 |
| 60 ans et plus | 17,4 | 0,3 | 9,6 |

**Putting a point of view**

You will hear a busy working mother extolling the virtues of shopping in a hypermarket. You always buy your fruit and vegetables at the local market. Say why.

Mention that you like your produce fresh, you value the personal contact with the tradesmen and that you meet friends at the market. Supermarkets are too impersonal. You do not like being watched by hidden cameras and having to listen to canned music. Besides there are so many things on offer, you usually buy more than you need.

**Description**

Describe the picture overleaf. There are questions on the tape to help you to do so. Answer them first and then talk about the picture a second time without the stimulus of the questions.

# 2
# Reading

## Techniques for improvement of reading skills

There is a simple way to improve your understanding of the written word – read as widely as possible and do so on a regular basis. Set aside a period of time each day for reading something in French. It may be directly connected with your course – a set book or a topic – or it may be a favourite author, or an article from a newspaper or a magazine. The more you read the wider your passive vocabulary will become and the easier it will be to understand the gist of what you are reading.

Resist the temptation to look up every new word in the dictionary. Besides being time consuming, the enjoyment of reading will soon be killed. If you learn to recognize and understand the key elements in a sentence, you will comprehend the basic message. This is the first step towards gist comprehension of a passage. Learn to pick out the subject, main verb and object in a sentence.

## Example

The short story 'Un Duel' by Maupassant begins with these words:

La guerre était finie; les Allemands occupaient la France.

These are simple, direct statements, easy to understand. Later, one of the main characters is introduced thus:

Monsieur Dubuis, qui avait fait partie de la garde nationale de Paris pendant toute la durée du siège, allait rejoindre en Suisse sa femme et sa fille, envoyées par prudence à l'étranger, avant l'invasion.

The key words here are 'Monsieur Dubuis' (subject), 'allait rejoindre' (verb), 'sa femme et sa fille' (object) and 'en Suisse'. The descriptive clause, 'qui avait fait partie de la garde nationale de Paris pendant toute la durée du siege,' and the phrase 'envoyées par prudence à l'étranger, avant l'invasion', tell us more about M. Dubuis and his family but are not essential steps forward in the story.

Understanding the key words in each sentence is crucial. If they are new to you, before reaching for the dictionary, try to derive their meanings by applying the following techniques:

(a) Decide what kind of word you are trying to decipher. Is it a noun, adjective or adverb? Nouns will probably be associated with an article (un, une, le, la, les, du, de la, des); verbs can be recognized through their tenses (look at the endings or the construction); adjectives will be the same number and gender as the nouns they describe; most adverbs end in 'ment'.

(b) Look for a connection with a known French word. Here is a word cluster based on the common word chaud (hot)

| | |
|---|---|
| chaleur (heat) | chauffage (heating) |
| chaud (hot) | |
| chauffer (to heat) | chauffé (heated) |

(c) Look for a similarity with an English word. Be wary, however, as some English words, although similar in spelling are different in meaning (des faux-amis!), e.g. 'Les assistants restèrent' does not mean 'the assistants rested' but 'the audience stayed'.

(d) The spelling of the word may help to reveal its meaning, e.g. words beginning with 'é' often begin with 's' in English

école – school        épée – sword

Words ending in 'ant' often end in 'ing' in English

nettoyant – cleaning        étincelant – sparkling

Words ending in 'eur' often end in 'er' or 'or' in English

danseur – dancer        docteur – doctor

Verbs beginning with 're' indicate a repeated action

redescendre – go down again

The suffixes 'in' or 'im' imply the contrary of the rest of the word

utile – useful        poli – polite

inutile – useless        impoli – rude

(e) If all else fails, guess, but do so in the context of what you already know.

Being aware of the subject matter of a passage, story or article, is the first step to understanding it and preparing your mind for the sort of vocabulary you will encounter. Passages set for comprehensive purposes

in examination papers are usually confined to one topic. Once you
have discovered the general theme, comprehension of the detail becomes
easier. Good French writing is noted for its classical elements of balance,
precision and logic. Like a formal French garden, where nature has
been trimmed, contained and arranged in neat geometrical patterns, so
is much French prose. A topic is systematically explored, arguments
for and against succinctly put and a logical conclusion drawn.

When studying articles from a magazine or newspaper, look first of
all at the lay-out. Titles and sub-headings are important although they
can be given a journalistic twist (designed to make them more
eye-catching) which can be misleading. The headline in particular is an
intriguing journalistic device.

Supportive visual material is a great aid to understanding the written
word. This may take the form of photographs, drawings, graphs or
pie-charts. Page lay-out is important. The reader's attention may be
drawn by putting certain sections in a box, printing more heavily, in
italics or a different colour, underlining, using capitals or setting apart
from the rest of the text. Decipher supportive clues such as these before
starting a study of the main text. They will help you to place the passage
in an intelligible context.

**Exercise A**

EN COUVERTURE

## <sup>vu de</sup><sub>2008</sub> L'Europe fait peau neuve

**Les tendances lourdes**

En 2008, les pays du Nord (Amérique et Europe)
ne représentent plus que 15% de l'humanité. Pour
25% en 1988 et 50% en 1914. Parallèlement,
l'actuel tiers monde s'achemine vers le record prévu
pour 2025 : au bas mot, 120 millions de Maghrébins,
dont 60 en Algérie; l'Afrique noire triple sa population; au Bangladesh, la densité atteint 1 524
habitants au kilomètre carré.

Non seulement l'Europe se vide, mais encore elle
vieillit. «Lors de la Révolution, observe Albert Sauvy,
il y avait en France cinq jeunes pour un vieux. A
partir de 2020, pour la première fois de notre
histoire, le nombre des plus de 60 ans l'emporte sur
celui des moins de 20 ans.» Et encore la France,

● **Qui
soignera nos
octogénaires?**

comme l'Irlande, n'est-elle pas la plus mal lotie. L'Italie, qui a tant essaimé dans le monde, et l'Espagne n'échappent pas à l'effondrement de la natalité. Le phénomène touche aussi le Japon: dans vingt ans, il sera, avec l'Allemagne, le pays le plus «vieux» du monde.

## Les conséquences

En France, Henri Guillaume, commissaire au Plan, estime: «Dans vingt ans, les retraites devront être amputées de 30%.» A moins, poursuit-il, de relever les cotisations ou de repousser l'âge de la retraite à 68 ans.

Mais surtout, selon Jacques Lesourne, il est illusoire de penser que le vide de l'Europe ne sera pas sans appeler des migrations. Il cite l'ancien président algérien Houari Boumediene: «Un jour, des millions d'hommes quitteront les parties pauvres du monde pour faire irruption dans les espaces relativement accessibles de l'hemisphère Nord, à la recherche de leur propre survie.» En faveur de cette prédiction: les communautés d'émigrés déjà présentes en Europe attirent de nouveaux membres; des troubles, des révolutions risquent d'agiter les pays surpeuplés et de forcer des millions d'individus à la fuite. Enfin joue le besoin d'une main-d'oeuvre pour soigner nos octogénaires...

## Les périls

L'afflux se produira-t-il sur un rythme lent ou rapide? Se bornera-t-il, en 2025, à 25 millions de personnes? Ou atteindra-t-il les 65 millions, auquel cas un Européen sur cinq viendrait d'Afrique ou d'Asie Mineure? La prospective se borne à envisager des scénarios. Le premier: l'assimilation possible en cas de migration lente. Pierre Chaunu recommande de bâtir en France des mosquées destinées à accueillir des musulmans qui se sentiront français. Second scénario, inverse: les immigrants, conservant, outre leur mode de vie, des liens étroits avec leur pays d'origine, se constituent en groupes de pression pesant sur la politique, intérieure et étrangère. La coexistence culturelle ne serait pas synonyme de coexistence pacifique; la haine raciale, la violence, le terrorisme auraient cours. «Hypothèse non négligeable en cas de migration rapide», admet Lesourne, sans exclure l'éventualité optimiste: la diversité, les mariages mixtes, l'influence réciproque

- **Un Européen sur cinq viendra d'ailleurs**
- **La RFA record de vieillesse**

> des cultures, l'émergence d'une culture islamo-
> européenne.
> Dans tous les cas, la vieille Europe est conduite
> à faire peau neuve. **M. L.** ■

1
  (a) What is the literal meaning of the headline?
  (b) What is the subject of the article?

2
  (a) If you are asked to make a résumé of the article in English, which French sentences, or parts of sentences, would you consider to be the most important? A 'hi-lighter' pen is useful for doing this.
  (b) Using these sentences as a basis, make a resumé of the article, in English, in less than one hundred words.

3 Read the first section (Les tendances lourdes). Give short answers to the following questions:
  (a) What will have happened to the population of Black Africa by 2025?
  (b) In Bangladesh what will be the population density in 2025?
  (c) What will happen in France in 2025 for the first time in history?
  (d) Which two European countries have the highest birthrate?

4 Read the second section (Les conséquences). Are the following statements true or false? If incorrect, put them right:
  (a) Henri Guillaume forecasts that contributions towards state pensions will have to be raised along with the age of retirement.
  (b) Jacques Lesourne states that we are deluding ourselves if we think that the empty spaces in the population of Europe will not be filled by immigrants.
  (c) The President of Morocco warned of an invasion of the poor of North Africa into Europe.
  (d) Euthanasia should be available for people over the age of 80.

5 Read the third section (Les périls). Fill in the blanks in the following passage:
  Will the influx of immigrants reach a limit of _____ in 2025? Or will it reach _____ in which case one European in every __ will come from Africa or _____? The assimilation of immigrants will be possible if migration is _____. However immigrants might maintain close ties with their _____ and form _____ groups which would influence both _____ and _____ politics. An optimistic outcome would be the emergence of an Islamic–European culture which would allow for _____, _____ and the _____ influence of the two cultures.

## Exercise B    Interpreting statistics

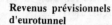

**Revenus prévisionnels
d'eurotunnel**

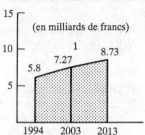

**Evolution du trafic transmanche et part d'eurotunnel**

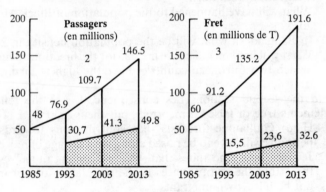

**Repartition du trafic eurotunnel**

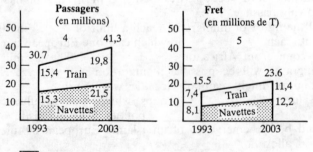

These graphs forecast the growth in use of the Eurotunnel.

1
    (a)   What does graph 1 forecast?
    (b)   What do graphs 2 and 3 forecast?
    (c)   What do graphs 4 and 5 forecast?

2  (Graph 1)
    (a)   How many francs are there in 1 millard?
    (b)   What is the revenue expected to be in 2013?

3  (Graphs 2 and 3)
    (a)   How many passengers are expected to cross the Channel in 2003?
    (b)   How many passengers are expected to use the tunnel in 2003?
    (c)   How many tonnes of freight will cross the Channel in 2013?
    (d)   What proportion of that (approximately) will be taken through the tunnel?

4  (Graphs 4 and 5)
    (a)   What is the total number of passengers using the tunnel expected to be in 2003?
    (b)   How many of these will be in motor vehicles?
    (c)   How many more tonnes of freight in lorries are expected to be carried through the tunnel in 2003 than are likely to be transported in 1993?

**Exercise C   Advanced Level**

There are many different ways of testing comprehension. Some examination questions have to be answered in French, as in this question taken from a paper set by the University of Oxford Delegacy of Local Examinations.

1
Remplissez les blancs dans ce résumé avec un mot qui montre que vous avez bien compris le texte. Vous pouvez utiliser des mots qui se trouvent dans le texte, si cela vous semble convenable. On a déjà rempli le premier blanc pour vous montrer comment.

Voici les résultats d'une **enquête** effectuée auprès de 216 médecins
_____. Presque _____ les médecins ont dû traiter le problème du surpoids parmi leurs clients, mais ce n'est pas \_\_ _____ pour des raisons esthétiques. Quelquefois, ils refusent de prendre en charge une demande, parce que celle-ci ne semble pas _____; pourtant, les trois quarts de ces patients sont traités personellement par _____ des généralistes. Normalement, on leur conseille de suivre un _____ avec ou sans _____.
Curieusement, une bonne proportion des médecins envoient ces patients voir un _____. Cependant, malgré l'importance qu'ils attachent

# Quand les médecins «font» le poids

Enquête *Le Point-Médical* réalisée auprès de médecins généralistes par Indice-Opinion - Indice-Médical (216 médecins interrogés).

La quasi-totalité des médecins (99%) sont confrontés au problème de surpoids dans leur clientèle, que ce soit à la demande des patients ou de leur propre initiative. Pour eux, conseiller (ou aider à) l'amaigrissement, c'est rarement pour des raisons esthétiques seules, mais pour éviter ou soigner des états pathologiques.

Le seuil de surpoids à partir duquel le problème est pris en compte varie suivant les médecins. Lorsqu'ils refusent de prendre une demande en charge, c'est le plus souvent parce qu'elle leur paraît injustifiée; 65% des généralistes disent assurer personnellement le conseil des trois quarts de ces patients; quand ils aiguillent vers un spécialiste, c'est surtout vers un endocrinologue-diabétologue (64%) ou vers un nutritionniste (16%). Les prescriptions portent essentiellement sur le régime seul ou associé à des médicaments (mais l'enquête ne précise pas s'il s'agit de médicaments «pour maigrir», ou de traitements pour des affections – hypertension, diabète, etc. – très souvent liées au surpoids).

Plus de 40% des médecins affirment avoir recours à la psychothérapie, associée éventuellement à des médicaments. Curieux! Sans doute s'agit-il là de ce qu'il conviendrait plutôt d'appeler un «soutien psychologique».

Une ombre au tableau: les réponses à des questions que nous ne reproduisons pas ici montrent que si les généralistes ont conscience de l'influence de l'alimentation non seulement sur le surpoids mais sur des pathologies variées, leurs prescriptions, en matière de régime, ne sont pas toujours adéquates. Responsable: une carence de l'enseignement de la diététique dans les facultés de médecine.

*Au cours de l'année écoulée, avez-vous été confronté(e) dans votre clientèle à des problèmes de surpoids?*

| | |
|---|---|
| Oui | 99% |
| Non | 1% |
| Ne savent pas | – |

*Lorsqu'il s'agit d'une demande de vos patient(e)s, quel est le motif de la demande?\** 

| | |
|---|---|
| Pathologie consécutive au surpoids | 17% |
| Perturbations métaboliques | 16% |
| Surpoids esthétique | 80% |
| Surpoids à retentissement psychologique | 43% |
| Ne savent pas | 2% |

*A partir de quelle majoration considérez vous qu'il faut prendre en compte un surpoids?\** 

| | |
|---|---|
| Plus de 10% par rapport à la norme | 37% |
| Plus de 20% par rapport à la norme | 38% |
| Plus de 30% par rapport à la norme | 5% |
| Quelle que soit l'augmentation réelle s'il y a une demande du patient | 19% |

| | |
|---|---|
| Jamais | – |
| Ne savent pas | 6% |

*De quelle nature est, le plus fréquemment, votre prescription?\** 

| | |
|---|---|
| Médicaments seuls | 1% |
| Psychothérapie seule | 1% |
| Régime seul | 31% |
| Régime + médicaments | 22% |
| Régime + psychothérapie | 32% |
| Médicaments + psychothérapie | 2% |
| Médicaments + psychothérapie + régime | 21% |
| Ne savent pas | 3% |

*Lorsque vous prenez en charge un(e) tel(le) patient(e), combien de fois le (la) voyez-vous en général?*

| | |
|---|---|
| Une seule fois | 1% |
| Deux fois | 9% |
| Trois fois | 19% |
| Quatre fois et plus | 59% |
| Ne savent pas | 12% |

\* *Total supérieur à 100. Plusieurs réponses étaient possibles.*

à l'_____, les régimes qu'ils suggèrent ne sont pas toujours efficaces, peut-être parce que l'_____ qu'ils avaient reçu n'était pas complet.

2

Pour chacun des cas suivants, donnez le **pourcentage:**

| | % |
|---|---|
| – des médecins qui n'ont pas dû traiter le problème du surpoids cette année | |
| – des patients qui consultent leurs médecins parce qu'ils n'aiment pas l'effet produit par le surpoids sur leur apparence physique | |
| – des médecins qui n'imposent pas de limites sur l'augmentation pour prendre en charge un surpoids | |
| – des médecins qui conseillent l'utilisation de médicaments pour les problèmes de surpoids (avec ou sans thérapies) | |

# 3
# Listening

Once you step on to French soil, or find yourself in a French speaking country, your ability to understand spoken French will be put to the test. Unless you are bilingual, you will find it difficult at first to understand all that is being said around you.

When people are speaking directly to you, understanding is made easier by the visual aids to comprehension which come into play – facial expression, body language and gestures. You can also ask for help.

> Parlez plus lentement, s'il vous plaît.
> Je regrette, je ne comprends pas.
> Voulez-vous répéter s'il vous plaît.

When you are in a crowd, however, listening to announcements or trying to pick up something on the radio, comprehension of the spoken word – listening in the abstract in this case – becomes more difficult. It can also be very tiring and do not be surprised if, at the beginning of your stay abroad, you wish to retire to bed earlier than usual!

If the ability to understand spoken French is the first skill to be widely used when in France, it is also the one to improve most rapidly. Certain words and constructions will become familiar through repetition; you will become accustomed to the local dialect, modern idioms, which may at first have been baffling, will become clear. Your aural comprehension will be greatly improved by the visit and the longer you stay the more progress you will make.

Many other sources of spoken French are available including: the classroom, radio, films with sub-titles, local native speakers, a French Circle and, of course, this book. The accompanying tape has examples specifically chosen to help you comprehend spoken French better.

**Techniques for the improvement of aural comprehension**

Be aware of what you are required to listen for. This is particularly important when doing listening tests in examinations. Always read the

questions carefully. You may be required to give a date, a price or a
time, so you will listen specifically for numbers. You may be asked for
a place or a position so understanding prepositions and the relevant
nouns is important. You may have to explain the reasons for certain
actions, so listen for words such as:

| | |
|---|---|
| parce que | because |
| à cause de | because of |
| afin (que) | in order (that) |
| pour (que) | so (that) |
| vu que | seeing that |

As with reading, understanding the key words and sentences is crucial.
Often there are linguistic markers to help you.

Words or ideas maybe stressed by repetition. This may take the form
of synonyms, explanations or different phraseology.

Speed and emphasis of delivery play an important part in drawing
your attention to an important section of the message. Voices may be
raised to stir your emotion and bring something important to your
notice, or lowered to take you into the speaker's confidence. Climaxes
also highlight areas of importance, particularly in formal speeches.

The context in which the words are spoken will help to focus your
attention on certain areas of vocabulary, e.g. a weather forecast will
employ a different vocabulary from that used in a train announcement.
The method of addressing one another in a formal situation differs
from that used in an informal one, e.g. conversations in the classroom
and the playground, or in the office and at home.

To improve your power of aural comprehension, listen to as many
different varieties of spoken French as possible.

## Practising listening comprehension

When we listen we use slightly different skills, depending on why we
are listening. The following examples of spoken French are recorded
on the cassette. By answering the questions in the exercises you will
develop your ability in this area.

### Exercise A  Listening for information

These two recorded extracts (*from an A/S examination set by the
Associated Examining Board*) will give you practice in gathering
information from spoken French.

Listen to each extract three times, answering the questions in the
book after each hearing before proceeding to the next.

1    Listen to the extract.
(a)    What is the cause for concern which has led to the launching of this campaign today?
Listen to the extract again.
(b)    What age are the children mostly affected?
(c)    What two Ministries are collaborating in this campaign?
Listen to the extract for the third time.
(d)    To whom is the campaign addressed?
(e)    Why is the phrase 'changeons de conduite' particularly significant?
(f)    Why are parents sometimes to blame?


2    Listen to the extract.
(a)    What is being advertised?
(b)    In how many volumes?
Listen to the extract again.
(c)    What three features are stressed?
Listen to the extract for a third time.
(d)    When does each volume appear?
(e)    How much does each volume cost?


## Exercise B    Reporting the spoken word

Taking notes in English on passages of spoken French is a useful and important skill. Secretaries able to report in English on meetings and conferences conducted in French are very valuable assets to a company. It is a skill required in many examination listening tests.

1    (*Question taken from an A/S level paper set by the University of London Examination Board.*)
In this extract (introduced as 'troisième partie') a French writer, Gilbert Cesbron, is being interviewed. Listen to the extract straight through first of all; read the questions and make notes on how you will answer them. Although your final replies will be in English, you may wish to note some phrases you remember in French. Listen to the extract a second time and supplement your notes during the recording. You are then given seven minutes to work up your answer in English.

## Questions
(a)    What is the interviewer's opinion of the works of Cesbron she mentions at the beginning?
(b)    What themes do they treat?
(c)    What is perhaps true about these works, according to Cesbron?
(d)    What statement by the interviewer is wrong, in Cesbron's opinion?
(e)    What comment does Cesbron offer about his other writings?

(f)   How does Cesbron react to the interviewer's comment that he has a following amongst the public?

(g)   What does he say in response to the suggestion that some people do not like him?

## Exercise C   Listening for pleasure

Many people find pleasure listening to music and/or the spoken word. French verse is unlike English poetry in that the language in which it is written is unstressed. There is, however, a rich and varied field of French poetry for you explore.

---

*'Ode' by Pierre de Ronsard*
Written in the sixteenth century, this short lyrical poem expresses the theme beloved of poets of all nationalities throughout all ages:

'Gather ye rosebuds while ye may.'

### Ode

MIGNONNE, allons voir si la rose
Qui ce matin avoit desclose
Sa robe de pourpre au Soleil,
A point perdu ceste vesprée
Les plis de sa robe pourprée,
Et son teint au vostre pareil.
Las! voyez comme en peu d'espace,
Mignonne, elle a dessus la place
Las! Las! ses beautez laissé cheoir!
O vrayment marastre Nature,
Puis qu'une telle fleur ne dure
Que du matin jusques au soir!
Donc, si vous me croyez, mignonne,
Tandis que vostre âge fleuronne
En sa plus verte nouveauté,
Cueillez, cueillez vostre jeunesse:
Comme à ceste fleur la vieillesse
Fera ternir vostre beauté.

---

*'Les Lilas et les Roses' by Louis Aragon*
Written four hundred years later, this poem captures the anguish, disbelief and shock at the swift and complete defeat of France in the summer of 1940.

### Les Lilas et les Roses

O mois des floraisons mois des métamorphoses
Mai qui fut sans nuages et Juin poignardé
Je n'oublierai jamais les lilas ni les roses
Ni ceux que le printemps dans ses plis a gardés

Je n'oublierai jamais l'illusion tragique
Le cortège les cris la foule et le soleil
Les chars chargés d'amour les dons de la Belgique
L'air qui tremble et la route à ce bourdon d'abeilles
Le triomphe imprudent qui prime la querelle
Le sang que préfigure en carmin le baiser
Et ceux qui vont mourir debout dans les tourelles
Entourés de lilas par un peuple grisé

Je n'oublierai jamais les jardins de la France
Semblables aux missels des siècles disparus
Ni le trouble des soirs l'énigme du silence
Les roses tout le long du chemin parcouru
Le démenti des fleurs au vent de la panique
Aux soldats qui passaient sur l'aile de la peur
Aux vélos délirants aux canons ironiques
Au pitoyable accoutrement des faux campeurs

Mais je sais pourquoi ce tourbillon d'images
Ne ramène toujours au même point d'arrêt
A Sainte - Marthe Un général De noirs ramages
Une ville normande au bord de la forêt
Tout se taît l'ennemi dans l'ombre se repose
On nous a dit ce soir que Paris s'est rendu
Je n'oublierai jamais les lilas ni les roses
Et ni les deux amours que nous avons perdu

Bouquets du premier jour lilas des Flandres
Douceur de l'ombre dont la mort farde les joues
Et vous bouquets de la retraite roses tendres
Couleur de l'incendie au loin roses d'Anjou.

---

*Extract from 'Le Mariage de Figaro' by Beaumarchais*
Figaro is one of the best known characters from French literature. His wit, irreverence and charm symbolize one aspect of the French character, 'l'esprit gaulois'.

Here he is twisting his master, the Count Almaviva, around his little finger, poking fun at the English and making us laugh at the same time.

*Extract from 'Le Mariage de Figaro' Act III, Scene 5*

**Le Comte**   J'avais... oui, j'avais quelque envie de t'emmener à Londres, courrier de dépêches, ... mais, toutes réflexions faites...

**Figaro**   Monsieur a changé d'avis?

**Le Comte**   Premièrement, tu ne sais pas l'anglais.

**Figaro**   Je sais God-dam.

**Le Comte**   Je n'entends pas.

**Figaro**   Je dis que je sais God-dam.

**Le Comte**   Hé bien?

**Figaro**   Diable! C'est une belle langue que l'anglais; il en faut peu pour aller loin. Avec God-dam, en Angleterre, on ne manque de rien nulle part. Voulez-vous tâter d'un bon poulet gras: entrez dans une taverne, et faites seulement ce geste au garçon (*il tourne la broche*), God-dam! On vous apporte un pied de boeuf salé sans pain. C'est admirable! Aimez-vous à boire un coup d'excellent bourgogne ou de clairet, rien que celui-ci (*il débouche une bouteille*): God-dam! On vous sert un pot de bière, en bel étain, la mousse aux bords. Quelle satisfaction! Rencontrez-vous une de ces jolies personnes qui vont trottant menu, les yeux baissés, coudes en arrière, et tortillant un peu des hanches: mettez mignardement tous les doigts unis sur la bouche. Ah! God-dam! Elle vous sangle un soufflet de crocheteur: preuve qu'elle entend. Les Anglais, à la verité, ajoutent, par-ci par-là quelques autres mots en conversant; mais il est bien aisé de voir que God-dam est le fond de la langue.

# 4
# Writing

As soon as you commit pen to paper or sit down in front of the word processor, you become aware of the fact that the end result of your labours will be fixed and in a form that can be read, studied and discussed. Accuracy, therefore, becomes important, correct spelling vital. Different combinations of the letters which produce the same sound must now be sorted out. For example, the pronunciation of the following four words is the same, but which is the correct word to use in each of the phrases a–d?

parler              parlez             parlé             parlai

    (a)   J'ai _____
    (b)   Je vais _____
    (c)   _____ – moi d'amour!
    (d)   Je _____

Any passage of extended French also demands that you pay more attention to the structure of the sentence. The hesitations, repetitions, unfinished utterances, recapitulations which are permissible (and sometimes even desirable) in spoken language, will not generally occur in the written form. When writing you have more time to marshal your thoughts and express them concisely in an effective manner.

Even if the written French consists solely of filling in forms or questionnaires (as required in some examinations), spelling is still important.

The rules governing the correct form of the written language make up its grammar. French, which evolved from the Latin spoken by the occupying Roman soldiers who, for four centuries administered Gaul as part of the Roman Empire, was codified and regulated in the sixteenth and seventeenth centuries after the invention of printing had stabilized the language. The grammar chapters of this book will help you to understand these rules. They do not present a complete, reference grammar, but rather a transitional grammar to show you how to know and use the correct written form when expressing your ideas on paper.

The ability to write French is tested in many ways in post GCSE examinations.

## Dissertation

This involves research and the writing up of a report in French. Time should not be a problem but do apportion it sensibly at the beginning of the course and stick to your deadlines. Choose a subject which interests you and for which there are readily available resource materials. Have an overall plan subdivided into more detailed requirements.

Make your notes in French. When you write them up use a good dictionary and reference grammar to ensure the accuracy of the French. Read the finished product carefully, checking for content, accuracy and style. Presentation of the dissertation is important. The work should be typed with a title page, table of contents, list of references and a bibliography.

A word processor is extremely useful for this type of work, not only for storing the information but also for producing the final draft and printing it.

## Essay

This is one of the classic ways of testing your ability to write in French. Whichever subject and essay style you choose, always make a plan in French before you start the essay proper and jot down some of the ideas and vocabulary you think you may use. Even if you don't use all this material, you have started the process of thinking in French which will carry over into your writing. Do not think first of an English sentence and then try to translate it. You will probably think of difficult, involved structures which will be difficult to put into French. Prose translation is a different exercise.

The vocabulary you use in an essay is not chosen for you by the examiner. You are bound only by your own limits. Write within your own parameters. The bigger your active vocabulary, the easier essay writing becomes, but do not think that to write well you must have the vocabulary of Flaubert. Making the most of what you possess is the key to success and a simple, direct style is often the most effective. As with the dissertation, check your essay for content, accuracy and the number of words.

Usually you are given a choice of subjects – discursive, imaginative, factual.

### Discursive essays

In this type of essay you are asked to discuss a particular subject. You may have definite views on this topic, but always make sure that you put down both sides of the argument.

The essay should have three sections. In the first paragraph explain what you understand the subject to be and how you are going to treat it. The main bulk of the essay will follow in which you give both sides of the argument. This section should be impersonal. In the final part state your preference and give the reasons.

Essays of this nature do not always have a single title and may require your reading some information before writing. When doing this note or 'highlight' important phrases.

Useful expressions for discursive essays:

| | |
|---|---|
| en revanche ... | in return/on the other hand |
| de l'autre côté ... | on the other hand |
| on peut dire que ... | one can say that |
| il est évident que ... | it is evident that |
| il faut dire que ... | it must be said that |
| en conséquence ... | consequently |
| à mon avis ... | in my opinion |
| je pense que ... | I think that |
| il est préférable que ... | it is preferable that |
| il n'y a pas de doute que ... | there's no doubt that |
| de toute façon ... | in any case |
| enfin ... | finally |
| en somme ... | in short |
| la possibilité existe que ... | the possibility exists that |

### Imaginative essays

These may take the form of straightforward fictional narrative or supposition ('What would happen if ...'). Be careful of the tenses you use in such essays as these.

Narratives set in the past will require the use of the perfect or past historic tenses and the imperfect; the story may be set in the future; suppositions will involve the use of a conditional tense.

Despite a possible tense complication, imaginative essays do give you the opportunity of displaying your own particular style.

### Factual essays

You may be tested on some aspect of your studies by having to write about a topic you have studied, under examination conditions. Prepare for this as for a dissertation, making all your notes in French.

## Letter writing

In everyday life we use written French most often in writing letters. Although business is largely transacted through the use of Fax machines and the telephone, formal business letters still have a rôle to play. There are set phrases you should use.

### Business letters

Formal business letters begin bluntly with:

Monsieur, Madame *or* Messieurs

They will end with one of these combinations, all of which mean 'Yours faithfully':

| | | |
|---|---|---|
| Veuillez agreér, | monsieur, | mes (nos) salutations les plus distinguées |
| Je vous prie d'agréer, | madame, | |
| Nous vous prions d'accepter, | messieurs, | l'assurance de mes (nos) sentiments les meilleurs |

If you have already met or corresponded previously with the person to whom you are now writing, you may start:

Cher Monsieur A *or* Chère Madame B

and end on a slightly less formal note such as:

Veuillez croire, cher Monsieur A, en mes (nos) sentiments les meilleurs

*or*

Veuillez accepter, chère Madame B, mes (nos) sincères salutations

Other useful expressions for this type of letter are:

| | |
|---|---|
| Nous accusons réception de votre lettre de ... | We acknowledge receipt of your letter of ... |
| Nous vous remercions de votre lettre en date du ... | Thank you for your letter of ... |
| Dans l'attente de vous lire, | Hoping to hear from you, |

### Personal correspondence

Don't throw away the envelope of a letter from a friend. It will have the sender's address written on the back. On the letter itself, only the name of the town from which it was sent will appear.

When writing a letter, be particularly aware of the difference between the ways of addressing people – 'vous', the more formal mode of address which is singular and plural, 'tu', the personal, intimate form which can only be used in the singular. Keep to the same person throughout the letter in all its forms, e.g.:

| | |
|---|---|
| Vous | Tu |
| Votre père | Ton père |
| S'il vous plaît | S'il te plaît |
| Venez chez nous | Viens chez moi |
| Vous | Toi |

There are several ways of signing off for this type of letter:

| | |
|---|---|
| A bientôt | See you soon |
| Ton ami(e) | Your friend |
| Amitiés | Best wishes |
| Grosses bises | Love and kisses |
| Comme toujours | As always |

## Dialogues

Using known speech patterns enables some candidates to write more freely. There is less of a tendency to construct elaborate, involved sentences. It is, however, not easy to write naturally in this form. Remember that the past historic (often a bogey tense) is not used in speech.

## Note-taking

This is a useful skill for preparing for, and taking, examinations and for wider use in the world of work. The ability to take notes in French, either for writing up in that language or transcription into English, can be improved with practice. The passage on the accompanying tape will help you to take notes from an oral source. Once you have done this use the transcript in the answer section of this book to check and amplify your work.

## Exercise A   Note-taking

Listen to the passage and make notes in French on what you think are the main points. Listen again and use the pause button on your tape recorder to enable you to make further, more detailed notes.

Listen a third time straight through and make any alterations or additions you think necessary. Use your notes to make a summary in French of the passage.

Finally use them to make a résumé in English. Compare your version with the transcript of the original in Part 7 (p. 216).

## Translation into French

The translation of a passage of English into French, prose composition, used to be a popular testing technique. It demands a thorough knowledge of the grammar of the language, a wide vocabulary and a need for accuracy. It remains a very effective way of testing a student's ability to write correctly and is still a component of many examinations, although no longer a major factor.

Before starting the translation, read through the whole passage and decide on the main tense you should use. Most mistakes are made in the translation of verbs, so think carefully of the tense and spelling of each one.

When the exercise is finished, check it carefully for avoidable mistakes. There is a check list in the grammar chapter entitled 'Helpful hints' which will help to eliminate this type of error. Apply it to any written piece of French.

## Dictation

Like prose composition, dictation has now dropped out of favour with examiners. It is, however, a useful exercise in careful listening and accurate writing. The dictation passage recorded on the accompanying cassette also practises translation into and from French.

The following terms are used in a dictation exercise:

| | |
|---|---|
| point | full stop |
| virgule | comma |
| en guillemets | in inverted commas |

## Exercise B   Dictation

The passage will be read three times in all – firstly at normal speed, then at dictation speed with each phrase being repeated, finally at normal speed. When you have finished check it with the transcript and translate it into English.

You can then play the English version which is read at dictation speed on the tape and retranslate this into the original French.

## Other writing tasks

Written responses may be generated from articles taken from newspapers, photographs, advertisements, tapes and videos.
They may include:

Cloze tests – filling in gaps in a passage of French
Translation into English
Rephrasing – expressing certain passages taken from a printed text in
a different way

## Exercise C

The following examination questions are taken from a paper set by the
Joint Matriculation Board for 'A' Level.

---

**Lisez attentivement les textes suivants, puis répondez aux questions.
Nous vous recommandons de passer au moins cinq minutes à la lecture
de chaque texte et de répondre aux questions sur le Texte A avant de
lire le Texte B. Nous vous conseillons de ne pas recopier mot à mot
des sections entières du texte.**

---

## TEXTE A

### *L'ordonnance antistress*

Un hiver à couper au brise-glace et un printemps plutôt frisquet:
il est temps de se refaire une santé en vacances.

Les vacances doivent tout changer: effacer les symptômes du
stress, liquider la vie harassante. Un Français sur deux part en
congés d'été pour une durée moyenne de vingt-cinq jours. De quoi,
normalement, transformer le citoyen moyen, maussade, épuisé et
blafard en un surhomme bronzé, assuré et dispos. Mais gare aux
pièges! D'innombrables estivants reviendront comme ils sont partis.
Voire plus mal. Car ils commettent bien des bévues. Ils se bousculent
par milliers au volant de leur voiture le même jour. Ils veulent se
reposer, mais s'éclatent dans les boîtes de nuit jusqu'au petit matin.
Ils désirent se donner bonne mine, et s'affalent des heures durant
en plein soleil, au risque d'y "laisser leur peau". Ils s'occupent de
leur corps, mais s'épuisent en activités physiques auxquelles rien
ne les a préparés. Profiter des vacances, c'est presque un art.

On se baigne et on bronze, on drague et on se défonce sur les
courts de tennis. Le soleil est un excellent médicament contre la
déprime. Et puis, bronzé on se sent beau, plus sûr de soi, bref,
mieux dans sa peau. Mais gare aux excès, car comme tout
changement dans le rythme de vie, les vacances occasionnent un
stress.

Préparez donc votre départ, ne faites pas vos achats à la dernière
minute. Cette contrainte s'ajouterait à la fatigue d'une année de
travail. Prenez plutôt un temps de répit à la maison pour vous
détendre, et vous éviterez également l'énervement des embouteillages sur les routes.

Si vous choisissez malgré tout de partir, dès le premier jour de vos congés, au volant de votre voiture, faites de nombreuses pauses et des mouvements de relaxation. Soyez positif! Comptez les kilomètres que vous avez parcourus et non la distance qui vous reste à parcourir.

Ne cédez pas à la tentation d'une alimentation trop riche. La "bonne bouffe" conviviale fait plaisir. Quotidienne, elle stresse l'organisme. Redressez au contraire les égarements de l'année, mangez plus de fruits et de légumes.

---

1   (a) D'après le Texte A, quel devrait être en principe le rôle des vacances?

(b) Trouvez dans le texte **trois** conseils que le vacancier doit suivre pour éviter le stress.

(c) Lequel de ces conseils vous semble le plus important? Expliquez pourquoi en 50 mots environ.

(d) Vous cherchez des vacances antistress. Formulez **cinq** questions que vous poseriez à un agent de voyages pour vous permettre de faire un bon choix.

2   Traduisez en anglais le deuxième paragraphe du Texte A *(Les vacances doivent tout changer ... Profiter des vacances, c'est presque un art)*.
**Ecrivez toutes les deux lignes.**

3   Le passage qui suit est pris dans une autre partie de l'article d'où est tiré le Texte A. Faites une liste des mots qui manquent. Utilisez les mots et les expressions ci-dessous. Mais attention! Vous ne les utiliserez pas tous.

Vous voulez être content de vos vacances? Eh bien! Suivez ces conseils!
Pour ... (a) ... vos vacances, évitez l'isolement. Ne vous coupez pas de votre ... (b) ... de soutien, famille et amis. Il faut que vous ... (c) ... avec ceux que vous connaissez bien, car la cohabitation peut vous ... (d) ... Quand vous ... (e) ... d'arriver et ... (f) ... vous voulez sortir, ... (g) ... -vous des mondanités excessives dans les clubs, cela ... (h) ... vous coûter.
Vous ... (i) ... mieux de vos vacances si vous avez ... (j) ... toutes les questions en suspens (notes, factures). Fixez-vous ... (k) ... nouveaux objectifs personnels. Cela vous fera du bien. Mais, attention! En un jour de ... (l) ... physique ce bénéfice peut être perdu. Cependant, si vous êtes habitué ... (m) ... un train de vie trépidant, ne choisissez pas un endroit trop ... (n) ...

| à | méfiez | profiteriez | réseau |
|---|--------|-------------|--------|
| agacer | partez | que | réussir |
| animé | partiez | rajeunir | succéder |
| de | pourrait | réglé | surmenage |
| des | pouvait | répondu | tranquille |
| êtes venu | profiterez | repos | venez |

---

## TEXTE B

—Moi, monsieur l'inspecteur, j'ai durement travaillé pour obtenir les diplômes devant faire de moi le monsieur dont mes parents, petits ouvriers, rêvaient. Je me figurais qu'un labeur appliqué, l'amour du métier vous apportaient la considération des autres. Quelle erreur! L'échec entraîne le mépris, la réussite, la haine! Dès que je suis entré dans une usine, je me suis senti entouré par une hostilité vigilante qui cherchait à me briser en employant tous les procédés même les plus infâmes. Parce que j'étais le plus intelligent, les médiocres souhaitaient ma perte. Si je débitais la série des humiliations qu'on m'a infligées, des injustices dont j'ai été victime et qui permettaient à des gens n'ayant pas mon savoir de me dépasser dans la hiérarchie des traitements, je n'en finirais jamais!

Limogne écoutait cet homme se débattre avec ses propres démons qui, le harcelant, le maintenaient à l'écart de ses semblables. Le flot de ses rancoeurs se déversait sans répit. Le policier commençait à le comprendre.

—Par la suite, cette haine qui m'entourait sur mon lieu de travail a débordé dans la rue. Mes voisins se sont mis à me détester. Alors, ils ont tout inventé pour me rendre l'existence difficile; jusqu'à cet hôtelier qui dressait son chien à me mordre! Notez que je les méprisais assez pour ne pas me soucier de leurs vilenies, mais ma femme en souffrait.

Nous formions un couple merveilleusement uni, ma femme et moi. A cause d'elle, je supportais tout. Puis, Maria est venue. Une bénédiction du Ciel, cette petite fille. Je me fichais de mon avancement depuis que j'avais un enfant. Je me croyais assuré de l'avenir, désormais. Pauvre imbécile ... Cinq ans plus tard, ma femme mourait d'une pleurésie mal soignée par un médecin sans scrupule. Je suis resté seul avec Maria. Je lui en voulais de ne pas souffrir autant que moi de la mort de sa mère. Ensuite, au fur et à mesure que les années passaient, qu'elle remportait des succès, je la voyais s'engager dans la même voie que moi. Cependant, au lieu de nous rapprocher, cette démarche identique nous a un peu plus séparés. Elle osait penser que je n'avais pas été à la hauteur de ma tâche!

**4** Exprimez en vos propres termes ce que vous entendez par **six** des expressions suivantes.

Par exemple: devant faire de moi le monsieur dont mes parents rêvaient (1$^{er}$ para)

qui devaient apporter le prestige social que mes parents désiraient pour moi

(a) *un labeur appliqué, l'amour du métier vous apportaient la considération des autres* (1$^{er}$ para).

(b) *les médiocres souhaitaient ma perte* (1$^{er}$ para).

(c) *des gens n'ayant pas mon savoir* (1$^{er}$ para).

(d) *le maintenaient à l'écart de ses semblables* (2$^{ème}$ para).

(e) *qui m'entourait sur mon lieu de travail* (3$^{ème}$ para).

(f) *nous formions un couple merveilleusement uni* (4$^{ème}$ para).

(g) *je n'avais pas été à la hauteur de ma tâche* (4$^{ème}$ para).

**5** Traduisez en français le texte qui suit, en utilisant le Texte B pour vous aider. Vous pouvez employer ou bien le passé composé ou bien le passé simple.
**Ecrivez toutes les deux lignes.**

Jean and his wife had been married for five years when Maria was born. He himself put up with the hatred of those he despised, but their mean acts upset his wife. Eventually, she died and from then on the unscrupulous neighbours began to harass him and his daughter. Her fellow workers resented the success of Maria, whose future had been assured since she obtained promotion. Luckily, she and Jean remained indifferent to all this continual hostility.

# 5
# Literature

One of the most enjoyable benefits of learning French is that it opens the door to a vast new library of world renowned books. French literature, from Rabelais to Robbe-Grillet, reflects contemporary and universal values seen from the viewpoint of a people which has always respected its culture and traditions. Even if the course you are following does not contain a literature option, read something from the French classics. The paperback series 'Les Livres de Poche' provides plenty of good books at a reasonable price.

If you are not used to reading anything as long as a novel, approach the task gradually. Start off with short stories. 'Les Contes de Maupassant' (often set books themselves) provide an excellent introduction to French literature.

Read for the pleasure of reading. Do not worry about the meaning of every word. Only have recourse to a dictionary if, at the end of a paragraph, you still do not know what is happening. Aim for a gist comprehension and keep going to the end of the story. If you persevere you will find that your comprehension improves, you read faster and you get more enjoyment from the activity.

Cartoons, 'les bandes dessinées', are considered by many French people as a form of art and can be a valuable source of pleasure through reading. The language may be difficult to understand either by being too colloquial or, as with Astérix, full of classical puns, but the supportive pictures are a great aid to comprehension.

## How to improve your performance in the literature examination

Examination questions based on information and ideas acquired through the study of literature fall broadly into two categories. Some books you are required to study in detail in order to answer precise questions set to test your knowledge of the events, characters and implications to be found in the book. Other books have been chosen as they can be linked to illustrate a certain theme or topic. For example, under the heading of 'La Guerre', set by the Cambridge Examination Board, the following books are recommended reading:

Boule de Suif et Autres Contes de la Guerre – Maupassant
Pilote de Guerre – Saint Exupéry
An Anthology of Second World War French Poetry – Methuen
Un Sac de Billes – Joffo

Between them, these books cover the three major wars France has suffered since 1870. Questions asked on this particular topic are not limited to one book, but require a knowledge of all four. You would do well to read other books on the same theme, e.g. 'La Peste' (Camus) which gives insight into the feelings of many French people during the occupation of France from 1940–1944.

Not all themes set have a literary base and they are regularly changed. The syllabus of the examination gives details of the required reading.

The study of specific set books does not eliminate the need for background reading. Always read around the book you are required to study. Knowing something of the time at which the book was written, the nature of the society, its values and standards, events in the author's life which may be reflected in his/her writing, etc., will help in the appreciation of the work. Read other literature written at the same time so that you can compare your set author with other writers, and in so doing probably discover why his/her book was picked for study.

The set book should be read at least three times. The first reading should be swift with the principal objective of understanding the story. Next, do your background reading and embark on a detailed study of the text. Finally read straight through again, preferably after a lapse of some weeks or just before the examination to refresh your memory and perhaps revise your ideas.

Preparing to answer questions based on books requires taking notes. If your answers are to be written in English, make notes in English, if they are to be written in French, take notes in French. Make a summary of the plot in note form, analyse the major characters, identify the theme (or themes) running through the work. Illustrate your remarks with events and quotes taken from the book. It is useful practice to write these physically side by side so that, if you make a comment, you can see the supporting evidence. These notes are invaluable when revising for examinations.

Picking relevant passages to illustrate examination answers is an art. After the third reading of the text you should be able to identify the critical moments in the story or the play. Look here for suitable quotes to learn by heart. People reveal their true characters in moments of tension, so look here for quotations to use when discussing character. Even if you are allowed to take set books into the examination with you (as is sometimes the case) make a note of where the crisis points are so that you can find them quickly.

## Examination pointers

1   Make a plan of your answer. Jot down in note form the line of your argument and any relevant quotes.
2   Substantiate every statement with incidents and/or quotations taken from the text.
3   Stick to the point!
4   Do not just recapitulate the plot.
5   Incidents taken from the text can be quoted out of order provided they justify your remarks.
6   Avoid being irrelevant just so that you can drag in a quotation you have learnt by heart and don't want to waste.
7   Don't equate length with quality. Short, relevant answers are better than long, rambling ones.
8   Apportion your time sensibly and don't spend too long on one question.
9   If you are running short of time, write the last answer in note form.
10   Don't panic!

Although the idea of studying literature may seem a difficult task which should be avoided at all costs if an alternative exists, do not let this deter you from considering this option. Experience has shown that, for many students who started the literature course with misgivings, it proved to be in the end the most enjoyable part of their studies.

## Example

The following extract is from 'Vol de Nuit' by Antoine de Saint-Exupéry (1900–1944), a pioneer airman, who described the dangers and heroism of those early fliers in memorable prose.
   The extract is treated:
(a)   as a context question (answer in French);
(b)   for its wider significance (answer in English in note form).

Il monta, en corrigeant mieux les remous, grâce aux repères qu' offraient les étoiles. Leur aimant pâle l'attirait. Il avait peiné si longtemps, à la poursuite d'une lumière, qu'il n'aurait plus lâché la plus confuse. Riche d'une lueur d'auberge, il aurait tourné jusqu'à la mort, autour de ce signe dont il avait faim. Et voici qu'il montait vers des champs de lumière.
   Il s'élevait peu à peu, en spirale, dans le puits qui s'était ouvert, et se refermait au-dessous de lui. Et les nuages perdaient, à mesure qu'il montait, leur boue d'ombre, ils passaient contre lui, comme des vagues de plus pures et blanches. Fabien émergea.

Sa surprise fut extrême: la clarté était telle qu'elle l'éblouissait. Il dut, quelques secondes, fermer les yeux. Il n'aurait jamais cru que les nuages, la nuit, pussent éblouir. Mais la pleine lune et toutes les constellations les changeaient en vagues rayonnantes.

L'avion avait gagné d'un seul coup, à la seconde même où il émergeait, un calme qui semblait extraordinaire. Pas une houle ne l'inclinait. Comme une barque qui passe la digue, il entrait dans les eaux réservées. Il était pris dans une part de ciel inconnue et cachée comme la baie des îles bienheureuses. La tempête, au-dessous de lui, formait un autre monde de trois mille mètres d'épaisseur, parcouru de rafales, de trombes d'eau, d'éclairs, mais elle tournait vers les astres une face de cristal et de neige.

Fabien pensait avoir gagné des limbes étranges, car tout devenait lumineux, ses mains, ses vêtements, ses ailes. Car la lumière ne descendait pas des astres, mais elle se dégageait, au-dessous de lui, autour de lui, de ces provisions blanches.

Ces nuages, au-dessous de lui, renvoyaient toute la neige qu'ils recevaient de la lune. Ceux de droite et de gauche aussi, hauts comme des tours. Il circulait un lait de lumière dans lequel baignait l'équipage. Fabien, se retournant, vit que le radio souriait.

— Ça va mieux! criait-il.

Mais la voix se perdait dans le bruit du vol, seuls communiquaient les sourires. 'Je suis tout à fait fou', pensait Fabien, 'de sourire: nous sommes perdus.'

Pourtant, mille bras obscurs l'avaient laché. On avait dénoué ses liens, comme ceux d'un prisonnier qu'on laisse marcher seul, un temps, parmi les fleurs.

'Trop beau' pensait Fabien. Il errait parmi des étoiles accumulées avec la densité d'un trésor, dans un monde ou rien d'autre, absolument rien d'autre que lui, Fabien, et son camarade, n'était vivant. Pareils à ces voleurs des villes fabuleuses, murés dans la chambre aux trésors dont ils ne sauront plus sortir. Parmi des pierreries glacées, ils errent, infiniment riches, mais condamnés.

Question 1: Situez cet extrait dans le livre 'Vol de Nuit'.
Answer: Le pilote Fabien, accompagné d'un radiotélégraphiste, conduit l'avion qui porte le courrier de Patagonie. Un orage a déferlé sur l'Argentine et le pilote s'est perdu. Il a réussi à s'élever au-dessus des nuages en montant vers des étoiles qu'il a vues dans une déchirure de la tempête. Il arrive dans cette zone lumineuese et sereine et, lui-même entouré de lumière, il sent un moment de joie sublime. Mais il sait qu'il est toujours perdu et tôt ou tard, quand l'essence lui manquera, il sera obligé de descendre dans la tempête qui l'anéantira.

Question 2: What is the significance of this passage?

Answer:

(a)  Illustrates the danger run by early fliers – lost radio contact, lost way, bad weather.

(b)  Bravery of aviators – no signs of panic, exchange of smiles, knowledge and acceptance of fate.

(c)  Nature of hero according to Saint-Exupéry – alone, man of action, stoic.

(d)  Setting complements the conception of hero – apart, above the clouds, surrounded by light.

(e)  Style – close observation from personal experience ('et les nuages perdaient ...'), lyricism and balance ('comme un barque ...'), apt similes (like thieves locked in a treasure chamber), concise and powerful (last sentence).

(f)  Wider significance – presaging his own death? (Saint-Exupéry himself died mysteriously on a dangerous mission over France.)

# 6
# Topic work

Most of the topics set for study fall under the general heading of 'Civilization', and they embrace many aspects of French life. They include contemporary issues (women's rights, the environment, violence in society), French politics, the educational system, the media, the arts, films, and the history and geography of France. The source material, as described by the Examination Boards, is equally varied. Information may be gathered from books, magazines, pamphlets, advertising material, newspapers, foreign and English television and radio, home-made recordings and commercially produced packages.

The way in which you organize your reading, listening and viewing, record and file your notes and store your material is important. The more systematic you are, the better will be the final result.

Although the syllabus of the examination may give you the names of books and articles to read, getting hold of them may be difficult. The most useful source of information is CILT (Centre for Information on Language Teaching and Research).

You may also get help from the following institutions and organizations:

Institut Français du Royaume-Uni
Ambassade de France (Service Culturel)
Centre National de Documentation Pédagogique
BBC Enterprises Ltd
Thames Television International

The addresses of all these organizations are to be found in Part 4.

Many magazines have special student subscription rates (abonnements). If you take one out, issues will be delivered regularly to your door. The following will keep you up to date and give you informed opinions on contemporary events in France:

L'Express          Le Nouvel Observateur          Le Point

Satellite television means that French TV programmes can now be picked up as easily as radio programmes. Recording facilities for both these media are highly desirable. Edit the programmes carefully; it is easy to become over-burdened with irrelevant material.

Conscientious preparation for a topic entails a lot of work, but all of it is useful practice toward your overall objective – improving your command of the language and your knowledge of France and the people who live there.

## A selection of topics set at advanced level

**Oxford**  (Resource packs available)
Aspects de la Politique ou des Actualités Françaises
Les Médias et la Communication
Les Arts en France
Une Région ou une Ville de France

**AEB**
L'Année 19__ (the year preceding the examination)
L'Urbanisme en France
L'Enseignement Primaire et Secondaire en France
François Truffaut

**London**
Quelques Problèmes Contemporains en France
La Sociologie des Loisirs en France
Régions et Régionalisme
Le Mode de Vie des Français

**Cambridge**
Le Commerce
Le Monde Francophone
Le Sport
La Religion

# Part Two
# Using French

For some students the challenge of learning a new language is sufficient reward for all the hard work involved. Most people, however, seek more than a purely intellectual satisfaction and use their hard won skill for pleasure or for work. Whatever the reason for learning French, being able to speak and understand the language well will always make any visit to the country more profitable and enjoyable. This part will help you to exploit your language skills.

# 7
# French for pleasure

## Travel tips

Before travelling take out a personal insurance policy and obtain a form E111 from your local post office.

## Air

Nearly twenty carriers operate from the United Kingdom to major French cities. Most of them will fly to Paris.

The French domestic airline, Air Inter, provides an extensive cover which links all the large towns in France. It operates 350 flights a day.

## Fly–drive

This enables you to hire a car ready for your arrival. The car is booked when you buy your ticket.

## Plane and train

A link between Air France and French Railways offers an attractive travel package. It can also be taken out with the SNCF 'France Vacances Pass'.

## Le fly France pass

This combined Air France–Air Inter ticket is available to young people under 25 or students under 27. It gives 4 or 7 days unlimited air travel in one month.

## Rail travel

The French railway system, rebuilt after 1945, boasts the 300 km/h TGV and an enviable reputation for reliability, comfort and service. If you decide to travel by train, see if you can use any of the following concessionary fares.

### Carte kiwi
Valable un an, la carte kiwi permet à l'enfant de moins de 16 ans et à ceux qui l'accompagnent (une personne au moins et quatre au plus) de voyager en 1er ou 2e classe avec 50% de réduction pour tout trajet commencé en période bleue.

### Carte couple
50% de réduction pour la 2e personne figurante sur la carte, la premierè personne payant le plein tarif. Il suffit de commencer chaque trajet en période bleue.

### Carissimo
Valable 1 an pour les jeunes de 12 à 25 ans qui voyagent seuls ou avec deux, trois ou quatre amis en profitant des mêmes avantages en 1$^{er}$ ou en 2$^e$ classe dans tous les trains sauf TGV. Il y a une réduction de 50% en période bleue ou 20% en période blanche. Carissimo vous permet d'avoir 4 ou 8 trajets réduits.

### Billet séjour
25% de réduction pour un parcours aller et retour ou circulaire totalisant au moins 1000 km. Il suffit de commencer chaque trajet en période bleue.

### Carte vermeil
Valable 1 an, la carte s'adresse à toute personne âgée d'au moins 60 ans quelle que soit sa nationalité. 50% de réduction en période bleue dans tous les trains en 1$^{er}$ ou 2$^e$ classe.

### Carte vermeil quatre temps
Valable pur 4 trajets simples. 50% de réduction.

### Carte vermeil plein temps
Valable pur un nombre illimité de voyages. Elle s'adresse au 'Seniors' qui pensent voyager très souvent.

La Carte RES (Rail Europe Senior Card) est inclus avec la Carte vermeil, vous donnant une réduction de 30% sur les parcours internationaux.

(For the above concessions choose your time of travel from a blue period which is generally Saturday 12.00 to Sunday 15.00 and Monday 12.00 to Friday 12.00, but check!)

### France vacances pass
This ticket gives unlimited train travel on 4 days out of 15, or 9 days out of one month.

For further information phone 071–834 2345.

*Train + auto*
Book a hire car at the same time as you buy a rail ticket. This service is available in about two hundred stations.

*Train + vélo*
Bikes can be hired at 241 French stations. They may be booked when you buy your ticket.

*Motorail*
If you have a long journey and short holiday, sending your car by rail will be quicker, more relaxing and could turn out to be cheaper.

## Road

If you are going by car, carry a red warning triangle and a spare set of bulbs and adjust the headlight beams for right-hand drive. The minimum age for driving in France is eighteen.

Most French main roads (routes nationales) date back to Roman times. Modern toll motorways are good, fast, not usually crowded but expensive.

'Priorité à droite' applies in built-up areas as well as in the country. Give way to traffic on a roundabout just as you would in the UK.

'Rappel' is a reminder that you are still in a restricted area.

Avoid travelling in peak holiday periods in particular:
15th July; 30th and 31st July; 15th August; 30th and 31st August;

*Speed limits*

|                    | Dry roads | Wet roads |
| ------------------ | --------- | --------- |
| Motorways          | 130 km/h  | 110 km/h  |
| Dual carriageways  | 110 km/h  | 100 km/h  |
| Other roads        | 90 km/h   | 80 km/h   |
| Towns              | 50 km/h   | 50 km/h   |

There is a minimum speed limit of 80 km/h for the outside lane on motorways during daylight on level ground and with good visibility. 'Les Anges de la Route' (speed cops) can fine you on the spot if you are breaking the law.

## Sea

If you can choose the time of day and month of the year, the cost of crossing the Channel by ferry can be much reduced. For many people, holidays really begin once aboard a ship.

## Hovercraft and Seacat

Links with rail and coach services provide attractive, quick ways of crossing the Channel.

## Channel Tunnel

This will provide the fastest access for motor vehicles to the Continent. Other advantages:
>    a quick passage through customs (once only)
>    a Channel crossing of 35 minutes
>    continuous 24-hour operation
>    frequent shuttle service for all types of vehicles
>    rapid, direct train travel from the heart of London to the centre of
>        Brussels and Paris

## Accommodation

Make use of the local Syndicat d'Initiative or Office de Tourisme for information about where to stay and what kind of accommodation is available. If it happens to be an Accueil de France tourist office, you can make same day hotel reservations (or up to 8 days in advance) if you call personally.

## Loisirs–accueil

This is an officially backed booking service for all types of accommodation.

## Gîtes

Self-catering holidays are popular and reasonably priced. The official London booking service, Gîtes de France Ltd, has over 2000 residences on its books. Telephone 071–493 3480 or write to the French Government Tourist Office for further information.

## Chambres d'hôtes

These offer bed and breakfast accommodation. They are an offshoot of the Gîtes de France organization. The residences are rural, mostly on small farms.

## Logis de France and Auberges de France

These one or two star, family run hotels are found throughout France with the exception of Paris. The 'patron', proud of his establishment, will do his best to provide a friendly service and regional food of a high standard.

## Auberges de jeunesse

Besides offering cheap accommodation to the young (and not so young), many youth hostels run courses for a wide variety of activities. For example, a youth hostel in the mountains runs courses in climbing, paragliding, moto cross, canoeing, tennis and hang-gliding.

## Camp sites

These abound in France. There are over 11,000 officially graded sites in the French Federation of Camping and Caravaning. If the English invented camping, the French made it into an art!

## Holiday activities

Because of its size, variation in geographical features, rural charm, modern cities, gastronomic reputation and sense of history, France has something to offer all holidaymakers. With a good command of the language, you can explore some of the more unusual aspects of French life and visit the places off the usual tourist track.

### Canal holidays

*Laze your days away!*
De l'Atlantique à la Méditerranée, prenez le temps de vivre au rythme des bateliers, en navigant sur les Canaux du Midi.

Des prestigieux vignobles du Bordelais aux étendues sauvages de la Camargue, vous serez séduits par l'art de vivre des habitants, par l'incomparable luminosité du Midi, par les cités chargées d'histoire telles Bordeaux, Agen, Toulouse, Moissac, Carcassonne, Narbonne, Aigues-Mortes ... et par les paisibles paysages traversés, bordés de cyprès, de platanes, de vignes, de vergers ou de champs de tournesols.

Pendant votre croisière, prenez le temps de goûter à la gastronomie locale: les coquillages de l'Etang de Thau, le cassoulet de Castelnaudary ou de Toulouse, les pruneaux d'Agen ...

Le Midi c'est aussi le pays de la fête. Festivals et réjouissances vous accompagnent tout au long du voyage.

For further information send to this address:

> Editions du Plaisancier,
> B P 27,
> F 69641 Caluire,
> Cédex

## Roads of History

*'Heritage Trails' – historic castles, abbeys, towns and villages – routes in various parts of France.*

La découverte d'un patrimoine aussi riche, aussi varié et quelquefois bien caché, comme celui dont bénéficie la France, a besoin de guides pour que la promenade ne devienne pas une simple errance un peu aventureuse ou égarée.

La Caisse Nationale des Monuments Historiques et des Sites, la Direction du Tourisme, la Demeure Historique ont perçu très tôt cette nécessité. Alors sont nées et se sont multipliées les Routes de l'Histoire. Elles vous feront voyager en plus de soixante itinéraires à travers la diversité des architectures, des grands aux plus petits monuments, de tous les styles: originalité du paysage français.

Beaucoup de circuits sont proposés, ils feront partager à tous la passion qui anime tous les acteurs de patrimoine aujourd'hui, pour que les décors de l'histoire d'hier puissent longtemps enchanter les promeneurs de demain.

For further information write to:
> Caisse Nationale des Monuments Historiques et des Sites,
> 62, Rue Saint-Antoine,
> 75004 Paris

## Loire Atlantique

Every region of France has its own particular appeal. Here are some of the attractions (known and not so well known) you would find if you spent a holiday in and around Nantes.

### La ville. Nantes, une capitale

Ancienne capitale de la Bretagne et résidence des ducs, Nantes est aujourd'hui métropole des Pays de la Loire. Dernier joyau de la Vallée des Châteaux, elle reste résolument tournée vers la mer. Sa haute cathédrale et son fier château Renaissance se dressent au milieu des vieux quartiers de la Juiverie, du Pilori ou de Sainte Croix. Ancienne 'Venise de l'Ouest' car rendez-vous des eaux, elle fut la demeure des coureurs de mers, armateurs et négriers et donna naissance au génie de Jules Verne.

### L'Hôtel de la région

The administrative headquarters of the region is a striking example of modern French architecture. It uses rose tinted concrete and glass to provide a functional, graceful building which harmonizes with its surroundings on the tip of an island in the Loire.

This is what the President of the Regional Council says about it:

La Région des Pays de la Loire existe aujourd'hui dans une double aspiration de ses habitants: solidarité d'où jaillissent des actions communes, enracinement dans des pays de longue tradition. Entre les départements, les communes et leurs cantons, entre hier et demain, la Région s'affirme comme le trait d'union indispensable.

L'Hôtel de la Region, symbole dans les bras de la Loire, exprime cet enracinement et cette solidarité qui fondent l'avenir.

### La Grande Brière
This is the second largest swamp in Europe and an area where it is still possible to enjoy moments of peace and tranquillity.

*Parc naturel régional de Brière:* Entre ciel et eau, à quelques lieues de l'ocean, s'offre un univers distinct, sauvage et étrange à qui veut bien tenter de percer ses secrets.

Monde amphibie aux immenses étendues de roseaux, pays noir couleur de la tourbe qui le compose, la Brière possède un capital humain et écologique exceptionnel. C'est au fil de l'eau, sous la conduite d'un Briéron, qu'il faut la découvrir, une flânerie en 'blin' à travers ce dédale de canaux, chalandières et curées restera inoubliable.

### Musée de la récolte du sel de la mer à Batz
Salt is still extracted from the sea by the time honoured method illustrated by the exhibition in the museum.

*Le sel de la mer:* Pays façonné par l'histoire et la main des hommes, les marais salants étalent leur étonnante marquetterie aux couleurs terre et rouille, décor géometrique ponctué de pyramides de cristaux blancs et de salorges noires.

### La Baule: station balnéaire luxueuse
With its enormous expanse of beach, La Baule is a mecca for water-sports' enthusiasts.

### Château de Goulaine
This family-run chateau has several attractions including guided tours, a butterfly farm and the chance to taste a classic Muscadet.

A 15 minutes du sud de Nantes, au coeur de son vignoble, Goulaine, le premier des châteaux de la Loire, est resté depuis près de 1000 ans entre les mains de la même famille.

### Angers
The city houses exhibitions of some of the finest tapestries in the Western World.

*L'Apocalypse:* Cette tapisserie illustre l'Apocalypse de Saint Jean. Elle fut commandée par Louis I$^{er}$, Duc d'Anjou, en 1375 et léguée à la Cathédrale d'Angers par René, son petit-fils. Elle montre le combat du diable et de ses bêtes pour l'âme des êtres humains.

La tapisserie inspira Jean Lurçat à faire son chef d'oeuvre 'Le Chant du Monde' qu'on peut voir dans le musée Jean Lurçat.

## Further information

For all information on holidays in France contact:
French Government Tourist Office,
178, Piccadilly,
London W1V 0AL
Telephone: 071–491 7622.

# 8
# French for employment

If you are going to apply for a job in France, understanding the advertisements might be your first hurdle. You will need to know the meaning of abbreviations such as:

| | |
|---|---|
| rech | required |
| SMIC | minimum wage |
| env | send |
| tél | telephone |
| expér | experience |
| BAC | Educational qualification (similar to A Level) |
| BTS, DUT | Educational qualification (Technical) |
| 150 KF | salary (150,000 francs) |
| hme | man |
| fme | woman |
| adres | send |
| écr | write |
| JF/JH | young woman/man |

You will also need to understand the expressions such as:

| | |
|---|---|
| exigé(e) | required |
| souhaité(e) | desirable |
| indispensable | absolutely necessary |
| disponible | available |

**Examples of job advertisements with comprehension questions**

### Exercise A

---

*DANS LE SECTEUR DES EQUIPEMENTS INDUSTRIELS,*
*UN MARKETING TRES TECHNIQUE*

Important Groupe Industriel Français (plus de 3 000 personnes; 1,4 Milliards de francs de CA), nous avons acquis depuis longtemps une solide réputation tant auprès des Industriels du Pétrole, de la Chimie, de l'Aéronautique que dans le secteur du BTP ou des Transports.

# JEUNE CHEF DE PRODUIT

(Débutant ou Première Expérience)

Vous développez et gérez une gamme d'équipements dont le marché se situe pour plus de 50% à l'Export.

Au sein de notre équipe Marketing, vous bénéficiez d'une assez large autonomie touchant aux domaines suivants:

- Analyses études de marchés.
- Suivi de la mise au point technique des nouveaux produits.
- Elaboration du plan Marketing et contrôle de son éxécution dans le cadre de la stratégie retenue.
- Assistance auprès des Forces de Ventes France et Europe.

De formation supérieure commerciale ou mécanique, vous avez une bonne connaissance pratique de la langue anglaise. A votre sens du contact, vous joignez des qualités d'animation et le goût du travail en équipe. Ce poste est basé dans le Centre de la France.

Merci d'adresser votre candidature sous réf.9618 à EURO-MESSAGES – BP 80 – 92105 BOULOGNE Cedex qui fera suivre votre dossier. Réponse et confidentialité vous sont assurées.

---

PARIS - STRASBOURG - LYON - MARSEILLE - BREST   *EUROMESSAGES*

---

1   In which fields does this firm operate?
2   Are they looking for a person with experience?
3   In which aspects of the job will you have quite a wide degree of responsibility?
4   Besides your qualifications, what extra skills or personal qualities are they looking for?

**Exercise B**

Société d'édition Paris 20ᵉ
recherche

**ASSISTANTE COMMERCIALE**

130 KF

(anglais exigé, allemand
souhaité) pour relations
et suivi fournisseurs,
clients, réseau de vente
et gestion des stocks.

Poste à pourvoir
très rapidement.

Adresser lettre manuscrite,

CV. et photo à

EDITOR CONSEILS
Att. Monique Heimfert

59, av. G-Claude, Z1 Les Milles
13290 Les Milles
AIX-en-PROVENCE

SOGINTER T.T.
recrute
pr longues missions et
déplacements à l'étranger
2 TECHN. BTS ou DUT
Electronique et mécanique
1 INGEN. PRODUCTION
bilingue anglais,
3 à 5 ans d'expérience.
123, rue du Fg- Poissonière,
Paris 9ᵉ.
ou TEL: 42.85.10.88.

SECRETAIRE
anglais nécessaire, pl. stable.
INGETEX, 10, r. du Mail.2ᵉ.

URGENT
filiale groupe
international, cherche
COMPTABLE
pour son siège centre
Paris
Très bon niveau
anglais exigé.
Contacter la ste BOEDELS
au 42.61.33.22.

1
(a) Which job requires a knowledge of English with German desired?
(b) Who would you be dealing with?
(c) What else does the job entail?

2
(a) Where would the technicians be expected to be posted?
(b) How many years of experience are required?

3
(a) Where will the accountant be working?

(b)   What kind of company will s/he be working for?

4 What qualities are looked for in the secretary?

## Applying for a post

You may be required to fill in a form and/or send a curriculum vitae (CV). How would you fill in this form?

```
Nom:
Prénom:
Adresse:
Age:
Date de Naissance:
Sexe:
Nationalité:
Marié(e)/Célibataire:
Enfant(s):                         âge(s):
```

Your CV should include these extra details:

    profession
    lieu de travail (place of work)
    expérience professionelle
    diplômes (include all your qualifications)
    stages (courses)
    langues parlées/écrites (the ability to communicate orally is important)
    disponibilité (availability)

When applying send also a handwritten letter explaining why you are attracted to the job, a photograph, stamped addressed envelope and two international reply coupons.

## Working holidays

If you wish to combine business with pleasure and take a working holiday in France, consult the book 'Working Holidays' produced by the Central Bureau for Educational Visits and Exchanges (CBEVE). This is available from the Central Bureau and most bookshops. It is updated every year and gives details of a variety of jobs lasting from 3 days to a year. Here are some of the jobs and areas of work from which you could choose:

domestic work (family and/or hotel)   work camps
archeological   grape picking   courier or rep   monitor   instructor

The CBEVE also runs a Junior Assistant Scheme for students between eighteen and twenty. This entails teaching for six months, usually from January to June. You would do twelve to fifteen hours a week teaching under supervision. Accommodation is provided.

The Central Bureau also provides details of study holidays and language courses held in France.

With an improved command of French the openings are there to take for enjoyment and profit.

Allez-y et bonne chance!

# Part Three
# A Transitional Grammar

'I gave him a "whatsit" in the "oojah" with my "thingummyjig".'

There could be several possible interpretations of the above sentence. Language, if it is to be comprehensible, has to be precise. When speaking, meanings can be made clear by using various devices like tone, gesture, facial expression, emphasis or repetition. With the written language, however, there is less scope and more care must be taken to get the form of words right, in order to express what is meant.

The written language has a series of rules to apply if it is to be expressed correctly. These form the grammar of the language. This part will help towards an understanding of the basic rules of grammar, point out the problem areas, link spoken forms to the written and lay the foundations for a closer study of French grammar.

Each chapter will have some exercises (the answers to which are in Part 6) to help practise what has been studied.

# 9
# Basic grammatical terms

'What's in a name?' Knowing the correct terminology makes life much easier, especially when studying grammar. Here are some of the terms you may come across:

NOUN: the name given to a person or thing.
      Examples:      boy          garçon
                  'plane       avion

ARTICLE: nouns are nearly always accompanied by articles.
      *Indefinite article*:      a        un, une
      Example:      **A** boy asked me
                  **Un** garçon m'a demandé
      *Definite article*:      the      le, la, l', les
      Example:      **The** train stopped
                  **Le** train s'est arrêté
      *Partitive article*:      some      du, de la, de l', des
      Example:      **some** cake
                  **du** gâteau

PRONOUN: a word which replaces a noun.
      Example:      The letter? **It's** on the table
                  La lettre? **Elle** est sur la table

ADJECTIVE: a word which describes a noun.
      Example:      An **odd** tale
                  Une histoire **bizarre**

VERB: a word which denotes an action.
      Example:      The lion **roared**
                  Le lion **rugit**

ADVERB: a word which describes a verb.
      Example:      He spoke **shyly**
                  Il a parlé **timidement**

SUBJECT: the person or thing that performs the action of the verb.

Example:                          **The centre-forward** shot ...
                                  **L'avant-centre** a lancé un coup ...

OBJECT: the person or thing upon whom/which the action of the verb is performed.
Example:                          ... and scored **a goal**
                                  ... et a marqué **un but**

DIRECT OBJECT: the person or thing which suffers directly from the action of the verb.
Examples:                         I saw **her** at the disco
                                  Je l'ai **vue** à la disco
                                  You threw **the stone**
                                  Vous avez lancé **la pierre**

INDIRECT OBJECT: the person or thing indirectly affected by the action of the verb. This usually involves the word 'to' in English.
Examples:                         I spoke **to her** at the bar
                                  Je **lui** ai parlé au bar
                                  We gave it **to the postman**
                                  Nous l'avons donné **au facteur**

DIRECT SPEECH: what is actually said.
Example:                          "Go away!"
                                  "Va-t'en!"

INDIRECT SPEECH: what was reported to have been said.
Example:                          He was told to go away
                                  On lui a dit de s'en aller

TENSE: the time at which the action of the verb took/will take/takes place.
Examples:                         I'll **take** two croissants          } *future*
                                  Je **prendrai** deux croissants        
                                  I'm sorry, **there's** only one **left** } *present*
                                  Je **regrette**, il n'en **reste** qu'un

INFINITIVE: The part which expresses the notion of the verb without giving it a particular subject or object. In English the infinitive begins with 'to'.
Example:                          I want **to swim**
                                  Je veux **nager**

PARTICIPLE: part of a verb. There are two forms, past and present.
Example:       We have **heard** the song of the nightingale } *past*
               Nous avons **entendu** le chant du rossignol    } *participle*

IMPERATIVE: form of the verb used to command.

Example: **Come on down!**
**Descendez!**

You will come across other grammatical terms in this book but these will be explained when you meet them.

## Exercise A

Des millions des sportifs absorbent des substances chimiques pour développer leur masse musculaire et la force. On paie des fortunes pour des anabolisants interdits par le Comité International Olympique. Le marché noir, tenu par des gangs de la drogue, s'est agrandi. Malheureusement, la police ne sait que faire.

1
(a) In the first sentence find 5 nouns.
(b) In the second sentence find 3 adjectives.
(c) In the third sentence find a past participle and a past tense.
(d) In the fourth sentence find an adverb and an infinitive.

2 Find the French for the following:
(a) the black market
(b) anabolic steroids
(c) body muscle
(d) sports men and women
(e) forbidden

3 Pour atteindre de nouveaux records sportifs, les drogues sont indispensables. Qu'en pensez-vous?

Discutez avec un(e) ami(e).

# 10
# Articles and nouns

## Singular

### Indefinite article (a, an)

*un, une*     These always precede the noun and show that it is singular.

'Un' indicates a masculine noun, 'une' a feminine noun.

Knowing the gender of a word is most important as it affects other grammatical forms, such as adjectives and pronouns. The accompanying indefinite article tells you the gender of a noun. This is the only really certain way of knowing. The endings of some nouns indicate their gender.

*Masculine endings*
    *-acle, -age, -eau* (oracle, sondage, bateau)

  Example:   - Regarde un ruisseau! C'est un miracle! -
          - Plutôt un mirage! -
          - Look a stream! It's a miracle! -
          - A mirage rather! -

*Feminine endings*
    *-çon, -son, -ion, -ette, -ée*
    (leçon, raison, action, serviette, arrivée)

Of course there are always exceptions to the rules.

*Grammatical poser*:  What do a high school, a museum and a mausoleum have in common?

*Answer*:     They all look feminine in French but are masculine:
         Un lycée, un musée, un mausolée.

**Definite article (the)**

| | |
|---|---|
| *le, la* | The singular forms denote gender. 'Le' denotes a masculine noun, 'la' a feminine noun. |
| *l'* | Before words beginning with a vowel or a silent 'h', le and la are replaced by 'l'' (e.g. l'habitant - the inhabitant). |
| N.B. | Some words begin with an aspirate 'h'; this is not pronounced but nevertheless the definite article does not contract to 'l''. |
| Example: | Le hibou est dans l'arbre près de la haie The owl is in the tree near the hedge |

## Plural

Both the articles and their accompanying nouns change their spellings in the plural. This change is heard in the article but usually not in the noun:

| | | |
|---|---|---|
| un, une | become | des |
| le, la, l' | become | les |

Listen to the article or accompanying word to tell you whether the noun is singular or plural:

| *singular* | *plural* |
|---|---|
| le frère | les frères |
| mon frère | mes frères |

Most nouns form their plural by adding an 's'. In the days before the advent of printing when manuscripts were copied by hand, an 'x' was sometimes confused with an 's'. Printing stabilized the written form and the alternative form of 'x' as a sign of the plural is found in many words, particularly those ending in 'u':

| *singular* | *plural* |
|---|---|
| eau | eaux |
| neveu | neveux |
| bijou | bijoux |

Words ending in '-al' change to '-aux' in the plural:

| *singular* | *plural* |
|---|---|
| cheval | chevaux |

'Z' is also a sign of the plural. Nouns ending in 's', 'x' or 'z' keep the same spelling in the singular and the plural:

le (les) bras

la   (les)   voix
le   (les)   nez

## Partitive article (some, any)

The partitive article denotes some or a part of the whole. Again there are different forms for words of different genders.

|  | *singular* | *plural* |
|---|---|---|
| *masculine* | du | des |
| *feminine* | de la | des |
| *masculine and feminine* *before a vowel sound* | de l' | des |

Examples:     du beurre, de la crème, de l'eau, des oeufs

Sometimes all forms of the partitive are replaced by 'de'. This occurs:

(i) after expressions of quantity
Examples:     une bouteille de vin, beaucoup de sucre
(ii) after a negative used to express an absence of
Example:     On n'a plus de pain

Articles are rarely left out in French. In English we often omit them:
Example:     I like tea or coffee in the morning and hot chocolate at night.
J'aime prendre **du** thé ou **du** café le matin et **du** chocolat chaud le soir.

The partitive article also translates ' of the ':
Example:     la femme du boulanger
the baker's wife

### Summary table of French articles

|  | Singular | | | Plural |
|---|---|---|---|---|
|  | *masculine* | *feminine* | |  |
| **indefinite** | un | | une | des |
| **definite** | le | l' | la | les |
| **partitive** | du | de l' | de la | des |

### Exercise A

1   From the following advertisement, pick out the nouns and their articles and translate them.

La voiture de votre choix. Vous voulez du luxe, du confort, de la vitesse? C'est ici. L'Hirondelle a tout ce que vous désirez:

- un moteur puissant et robuste (plus de pannes)
- des freins légers mais sûrs (plus de soucis)
- une ligne originale et élégante (beaucoup de coups d'oeil jaloux)
  Et tout ça à un prix imbattable!

2 Using the publicity as a model, write your own advertisement for a motorized bicycle called the 'Eaglet'. Features you should mention are:

> a cheap form of transport
> an economical engine (no more heavy petrol bills)
> reliable brakes (no more anxious moments)
> a simple, robust frame (no expensive gadgets)
> a reasonable cost.

*vocabulary*

| | | |
|---|---|---|
| vélomoteur | (m) | motorized bicycle |
| transport | (m) | transport |
| compte | (m) | bill |
| cadre | (m) | frame |
| truc | (m) | gadget |
| aiglon | (m) | eaglet |
| bon marché | | cheap |
| économique | | economical |
| inquiétant | | anxious |
| raisonable | | reasonable |

3 Read this advertisement, again noting the various types of articles. There are 4 indefinite, 4 definite and 2 partitive articles.

Découvrir une innovation indispensable est toujours un plaisir rare. Notre mémo-téléphone vous permet de prendre des notes, de dicter des lettres où et quand vous le décidez. Il vous offre aussi, une mémoire programmable, le rappel automatique des numéros occupés, l'indication de niveau des piles et un témoin de frais d'appel. C'est le goût de l'innovation et la recherche de perfection téchnologique.

4 Translate:

Discovering a new organizer is always a rare pleasure. Our mini-organizer allows you to dictate notes and answer letters when and where you decide. It gives you a huge memory, instant recall and an indicator of the state of the batteries. In the search for technological perfection it is a winner.

*vocabulary*

| | | |
|---|---|---|
| organisateur | (m) | organizer |
| gagnant | (m) | winner |

# 11
# Pronouns 1: subject, object, reflexive

Pronouns are useful tools of grammar which prevent unnecessary repetition.

## Subject pronouns

| Je | – | I | Tu | – | You |
|------|---|-------|-------|---|---------|
| Il | – | He, it | Elle | – | She, it |
| Nous | – | We | Vous | – | You |
| Ils | – | They | Elles | – | They |

Verbs change their spelling to suit the subject, but not necessarily the pronunciation, e.g. je chantais, il chantait, ils chantaient. The verb has the same pronunciation in all three cases.

There are two ways of saying 'you'. 'Tu' is the equivalent of the old English 'Thou' which has persisted in French. It is the personal form used only in the singular and when addressing members of the family, close friends and pets.

Swearing is also more effective in the personal, intimate 'tu' form.

Gender differentiation occurs in the third person singular and plural. With a mixed plural subject, the masculine form (ils) always takes precedence.

## C'est (It's)

This is one of the most common expressions heard in French. Usually it is followed by an adjective, e.g. c'est magnifique.

C'est is also used to define something (it's a ...) or to describe a thing or person when the gender of the thing or person mentioned is not known.

'Qu'est-ce que c'est?'          'C'est fantastique.'
'C'est un oiseau?'              'C'est un avion?'
'Non, c'est Superman. Il est formidable.'

## On (one, we, you, they)

This is another very common expression with a variety of meanings. It is often used colloquially instead of 'nous'. When 'on' is the subject, the verb is always written in the third person singular.

      Example:      On y va?
                       Shall we go?

## Object pronouns

These can be divided into two groups – direct and indirect. Direct pronouns are those which replace the person or thing immediately affected by the verb.

      Example:      I hit him
                       Je l'ai frappé

If the pronoun is indirectly affected and could also be expressed in English with the word 'to' in front, this is an indirect pronoun.

|  |  |
|---|---|
| Example: | I gave him a punch (a punch to him) |
|  | Je lui ai donné un coup de poing |

The difference between direct and indirect object pronouns in the third person must always be made in French although this need not necessarily be shown in English.

|  |  |
|---|---|
| Example: | I showed him the photo. |
|  | Je lui ai montré la photo. |

## Table of object pronouns

### DIRECT

| le | – | him, it |
|---|---|---|
| la | – | her, it |
| les | – | them |

### INDIRECT

| lui | – | to him, to her |
|---|---|---|
| leur | – | to them |

### DIRECT AND INDIRECT

| me | – | me, to me |
|---|---|---|
| te | – | you, to you |
| nous | – | us, to us |
| vous | – | you, to you |

### IMPERSONAL

| y | – | to it, to them, there |
|---|---|---|

### PARTITIVE
*(replaces all nouns preceded by du, de l', de la, or des)*

| en | – | of it, of them, some |
|---|---|---|

N.B. 'En' is often needed in French but omitted in English, particularly when the verb is followed by a number.

## Reflexive pronouns

|  | *singular* | *plural* |
|---|---|---|
| *1st person* | me | nous |
| *2nd person* | te | vous |
| *3rd person* | se | se |

Reflexive pronouns can be direct or indirect and behave like ordinary object pronouns.

Example:  Je me suis brûlé
*I burnt myself*

## Position of object pronouns

Object pronouns always immediately precede the verb except in a direct command.

Example:  Ton stylo? Je ne l'ai pas vu. Cherche-le dans ta chambre!
Your pen? I haven't seen it. Look for it in your room!

Should 'me' or 'te' occur at the end of the command they become 'moi' and 'toi'. Remember Carmen's warning:
Si tu m'aimes – regarde-moi, et si je t'aime garde à toi!

All pronouns, subject and object, when they follow verbs are connected to them by a hyphen.

When two object pronouns occur in front of a verb, there is a set order in which they must be used. The easiest way to remember this order is to think of them as being members of a team:

| *forwards* | *half-backs* | *backs* | *goalie* | *reserve* | *spectators* |
|---|---|---|---|---|---|
| me | | | | | V |
| te | le | lui | | | E |
| se | la | | y | en | R |
| nous | les | leur | | | B |
| vous | | | | | S |

Example:  La note! La compagnie dit qu'on nous l'a envoyée il y a une semaine. Où l'as-tu mise? Dans la corbeille? Tu les y mets toujours!
The bill! The company says it was sent to us a week ago. Where have you put it? In the bin? You always put them there!

## Exercise A
Match the phrases in Group A with the sentences in Group B.

### A
1  Les risques majeurs à notre planète
2  La température de l'atmosphère
3  La population du monde
4  Le trou dans l'ozone

5   Les déchets industriels toxiques
6   La destruction des forêts
7   Les pluies acides

### B

1   Elle augmente au moins de 80 millions par an
2   Ils menacent la santé des hommes
3   Elles dégradent 22% de la forêt européenne
4   Ils menacent la vie de nos enfants et de nos petits enfants
5   Elle contribue à l'effet de serre et à la disparition des dizaines
    d'espèces de plantes ou d'animaux chaque jour
6   Elle pourrait s'élever globalement de 3,5°C avant l'an 2050
7   Il apparaît au-dessus de l'Antartique

What are the major risks to our planet and what could be their likely
effects?
Discutez en français.

# 12
# Pronouns 2: relative, interrogative, possessive, disjunctive, demonstrative

## Relative pronouns

Relative pronouns relate, or join, sentences together by replacing a word common to both parts.

|  |  |
|---|---|
| Example: | I saw Pierre. Pierre was talking to Marie. |
|  | I saw Pierre **who** was talking to Marie. |

In English they are the words 'who', 'whom', 'which', and 'that'.
In French the most common relative pronouns are 'qui' and 'que'.
Which one is used, is determined by its function in the sentence. 'Qui' is used to replace the subject of the following verb, 'que' to replace the object. There is a rule of thumb which works most of the time. The structure of the sentence will help you. Remember:

|  | *'qui' + verb* |  | *'que' + noun* |
|---|---|---|---|
| e.g. | ... qui chante | but | ... que je chante |
|  | ... qui voit | but | ... que le garçon voit |
|  | ... qui révèle | but | ... que le journal révèle |

Both are used to replace people and things in the singular and the plural. 'Qui' is never altered, whereas 'que' becomes 'qu'' when followed by a word beginning with a vowel sound.

|  |  |
|---|---|
| Example: | Les experts **qui** expriment leurs opinions à la télé et les statistiques **qu'**il citent pour confirmer leurs idées, ne représentent pas toujours le monde tel **qu'**il existe en réalité hors du studio. |
|  | The experts who express their opinions on t.v. and the statistics which they quote to back their ideas, do not always represent the world as it really is outside the studio. |

In English we often omit 'which', 'that' or 'whom'. Always include the pronoun in French; in such cases it will always be 'que'.

> Example:       The car he bought is useless
>                La voiture qu'il a achetée est nulle

## Dont (of which, of whom, whose)

Be careful of the order of words in the French sentence when expressing 'whose'. 'Dont' must come next to the word it is replacing and be followed by the subject of the verb.

> Example:       The man whose son I know
>                L'homme dont je connais le fils

## Qui (whom)

'Qui' means 'whom' and not the usual 'who', when used after a preposition.

> Example:       La jeune fille derrière qui je me suis assis
>                The girl behind whom I sat

## Lequel, etc. (which)

To translate 'which' after a preposition use a form of 'lequel' which replaces the noun exactly in number and in gender.

|            | *singular* | *plural*   |
|------------|------------|------------|
| *masculine* | lequel     | lesquels   |
| *feminine*  | laquelle   | lesquelles |

> Example:       La boulangerie devant laquelle j'ai stationné
>                la voiture
>                The baker's in front of which I parked the car

You will also find these forms produced by a combination with the prepositions 'à' and 'de'. There are no contracted forms for the feminine singular.

| Masculine | | Feminine | |
|------------|------------|------------|------------|
| *singular* | *plural* | *plural* | |
| auquel     | auxquels   | auxquelles | – to which |
| duquel     | desquels   | desquelles | – of which |

## Exercise A

Rewrite these sentences, having joined them with an appropriate relative pronoun:

(a) Les Français aiment le foie gras. Le foie gras est un produit naturel.
(b) Mais horreur! On a trouvé des plumes de poule dans le foie gras. On a examiné le foie gras.
(c) Le foie gras vient du Périgord. On parle du foie gras.
(d) Les agents de la Répression des Fraudes ont examiné les blocs de foie. Ils ont trouvé des traces de plumes de poule dans les blocs.
(e) Le producteur accusé a dit "Nous sommes tous coupables." Ils ont parlé au producteur.

'La vache qui rit'

'L'oie qui triche'

## Interrogative pronouns (who? whom? what? which one?)

The forms of the relative pronouns, with the exception of 'dont', can also be used to ask questions. They will then come at the beginning of the sentence.

> 'Qui?' always refers to people and means 'who?' or 'whom?'
> 'Que?' refers to things or events and means 'what?'
> 'Lequel?' and its various forms refer to both and means 'which one?'
> 'Qu'est-ce que?' also means 'what?'

| | |
|---|---|
| Example: | Qui vous a accompagné au Palais? |
| | Who went with you to the Palace? |
| | Qui avez-vous vu? |
| | Whom did you see? |
| | Qu'a-t-il dit? |
| | What did he say? |
| | Qu'est-ce que qu'il a fait? |
| | What did he do? |
| | Laquelle des photos officielles préférez-vous? |
| | Which of the official photos do you prefer? |

**Exercise B**

Read this passage on the changing face of the French Riviera.

La Côte d'Azur possède une économie diversifiée qui contient un tourisme dynamique et une industrie tournée vers les hautes technologies. Les hommes d'affaires sont attirés par la Côte d'Azur qui a une forte concentration de palais de congrès. La région offre aux visiteurs d'excellents moyens de communication en constant développement. Pour les Français au moins la Côte d'Azur change d'image, et la région est devenue une des premières pour la création d'entreprises.

Ask these questions in French.
(a)   What does the Riviera possess?
(b)   Who are attracted to it?
(c)   What does the region offer visitors?
(d)   For whom is the Côte d'Azur changing its image?
(e)   Which of these changes do you like best?

Discuss the last one in French with a friend.

## Possessive pronouns (mine, yours, his, hers, ours, theirs)

As with 'lequel' there is a variety of forms to allow each noun to be replaced in number and gender:

|  | Singular | | Plural | |
|---|---|---|---|---|
|  | *masculine* | *feminine* | *masculine* | *feminine* |
| *mine* | Le mien | la mienne | les miens | les miennes |
| *yours* | Le tien | la tienne | les tiens | les tiennes |
| *his, hers, its* | Le sien | la sienne | les siens | les siennes |
| *ours* | Le nôtre | la nôtre | les nôtres | |
| *yours* | Le vôtre | la vôtre | les vôtres | |
| *theirs* | Le leur | la leur | les leurs | |

There are two groups for saying 'yours' depending on whether you address someone in the familiar form or not.
Note that 'le sien' can mean his, hers, or its.

**Exercise C**

1   To which of the following does each sentence refer?
        vélo    voiture    idées    bonbons
(a)   Nous avons donné les nôtres aux enfants.
(b)   Marie dit que le sien est plus petit.
(c)   Rien ne peut être plus délabré que la mienne.
(d)   Les leurs sont aussi intéressantes que celles de Galiléo.

2    Answer in English
(a)  What have we given to the children?
(b)  What does Marie have that is smaller?
(c)  Nothing can be more dilapidated than my what?
(d)  What do they have which are just as interesting as Galileo's?

## Disjunctive pronouns (me, you, him, her, us, them)

These are also known as stressed or emphatic pronouns. These descriptions exemplify their uses as they often draw attention to a noun and are always used away from a verb, i.e. disjoined or disconnected from it.

Often ownership can be expressed more easily by using 'à' + a disjunctive pronoun rather than the full possessive:

> Example:        Ce livre est à moi.
>                 This book is mine

|                | *singular* |   |        | *plural* |   |        |
|----------------|--------|---|--------|--------|---|--------|
| *1st person*   | moi    | – | me     | nous   | – | us     |
| *2nd person*   | toi    | – | you    | vous   | – | you    |
| *3rd person (m)* | lui  | – | him    | eux    | – | them   |
| *3rd person (f)* | elle | – | her    | elles  | – | them   |

*Uses*:
 (i)   After prepositions              *e.g.* Avec moi
                                       With me
 (ii)  To emphasize                    *e.g.* Toi, tu es un imbécile
                                       *You* are a fool
 (iii) After 'c'est'                   *e.g.* C'est vous qui l'avez dit
                                       You said so
 (iv)  On its own in answer to a       *e.g.* Qui a cassé la fenêtre? Lui
       question                        Who broke the window? He did
 (v)   When the subject of the verb    *e.g.* Mon mari et moi
       is split                        My husband and I

## Demonstrative pronouns (this one, that one, the one)

There are only four forms. They are always followed by a word or suffix.

|        | *singular* | *plural* |
|--------|--------|--------|
| *(m)*  | celui  | ceux   |
| *(f)*  | celle  | celles |

Followed by '-ci' and '-là' they mean this one (-ci), that one (là), these (-ci), those (-là)
*or*        the former (-là) and the latter (-ci).

Example:          Voici deux livres; celui-ci est plus petit que celui-là.
Here are two books; this one is smaller than that one.
L'Etranger et La Peste sont des romans de Camus; celui-ci est plus long que celui-là.
The Outsider and The Plague are novels by Camus; the latter is longer than the former.

Followed by 'qui', 'que' or 'dont' they mean 'the one' or 'the ones'.

Example:          Quels vélos? Ceux qui sont devant le garage
Which bikes? Those which are in front of the garage

Followed by 'de' they are used to translate the possessive "'s'

Example:          Ma voiture et celle de ma femme
My car and my wife's

## Exercise D

Pick out as many examples as possible of pronouns from the following dialogue. Say what they are and what they mean.

— Ce tee-shirt que tu as, ce n'est pas le tien. C'est celui que Maman a acheté pour moi hier.
— Qui t'a dit ça? Maman m'a dit de prendre celui-ci. En tout cas, le mien est trop petit pour toi.
— Que veux-tu dire? Maman, lequel de ces tee-shirts est à moi?

# 13
# Adjectives

Adjectives in French agree with the nouns they qualify. The majority add an 'e' to become feminine and an 's' to become plural. Pronunciation rarely changes in the plural and never in the singular if the final letter is a vowel. Adjectives ending in 'e' remain the same in the masculine and the feminine.

In many adjectives the change to a feminine form is more than just the addition of 'e'. Here are some common examples:

| -er | becomes | -ère | (premier | – | première) |
|-----|---------|------|----------|---|-----------|
| -if | becomes | -ive | (actif | – | active) |
| -et | becomes | ète | (inquiet | – | inquiète) |
|     | or | -ette | (muet | – | muette) |
| -eux | becomes | -euse | (heureux | – | heureuse) |

Some double the final consonant:

| -on | becomes | -onne | (bon | – | bonne) |
|-----|---------|-------|------|---|--------|
| -en | becomes | -enne | (parisien | – | parisienne) |
| -s | becomes | -sse | (bas | – | basse) |
| -el | becomes | -elle | (cruel | – | cruelle) |

As you might guess, there are plenty of exceptions. Here are some common ones:

| blanc | – | blanche | grec | – | grecque |
|-------|---|---------|------|---|---------|
| doux | – | douce | public | – | publique |
| frais | – | fraîche | sec | – | sèche |

Some adjectives ending in '-al', change the ending to '-aux' in the masculine plural:

social    –    sociaux

Although most adjectives follows nouns, some common ones precede:

bon         grand          mauvais          jeune          petit          joli

Three adjectives in particular need to be remembered, as they include a form used only in front of masculine singular nouns beginning with a vowel sound. This special form has developed in order to ease pronunciation and prevent a clash of vowel sounds.

| Singular | | Plural | |
|---|---|---|---|
| *masculine* | *feminine* | *masculine* | *feminine* |
| beau (bel) | belle | beaux | belles |
| nouveau (nouvel) | nouvelle | nouveaux | nouvelles |
| vieux (vieil) | vieille | vieux | vieilles |

> Example:   Que cet avion est vieux!
> Oui, c'est un très vieil avion.
> How old that plane is!
> Yes, it's a very old plane.

Adjectives are not always found next to the nouns they describe. No matter what their position in the sentence, they always agree.

> Example:   **La tomate** que l'étudiant enragé, qui ne pouvait plus contenir sa colère, a lancé au Ministre d'Enseignement quand il est venu faire un discours à la Faculté jeudi dernier, était **avariée**.

## Past participles

Past participles are parts of verbs and can never, in French, take the place of a complete verb.

> The past participles of -er verbs end in 'é'
> The past participles of -ir verbs end in 'i'
> The past participles of -re verbs end in 'u'
> The past participles of most -oir verbs end in 'u'
> The past participles of some irregular verbs end in 's' or 't'

> Examples:   parler  – parlé      finir    – fini
> vendre – vendu      vouloir – voulu
> prendre – pris      faire    – fait

Besides being used to form certain past tenses, they can also be used as adjectives and follow the normal rule for agreement.

> Example:   des feuilles tombées
> fallen leaves

When used to form a past tense, however, there are two different rules concerning their agreement.

If the verb is one of the few which takes 'être' to form the perfect tense, the past participle agrees directly with the subject:

      Example:          La dame est sortie
                              The lady went out/has gone out

If the verb takes 'avoir' to form the perfect tense, the past participle agrees with the preceding direct object (P.D.O.).

      Example:          La pomme qu'il a mangée était verte
                              The apple which he ate was green

Why is there a rule like this, and what can we do about it?

In languages such as English and French, word order in a sentence is important as this indicates meaning. The subject precedes the verb and the object follows, e.g.:

| *subject* | *verb* | *object* |
|---|---|---|
| The cat | ate | the rat |

Change the order of the words and it means something entirely different.

| *subject* | *verb* | *object* |
|---|---|---|
| The rat | ate | the cat |

If, in a French sentence, the order is upset but the sense remains the same and the verb is in a past tense involving a past participle, that change is shown by making the past participle and the object agree.

There are occasions when the object comes before the verb. The following sentence, for example, has the parts of speech in the standard order (subject – verb – object): *Jean a fermé la porte*. If the order changes and the object precedes the verb then the ending of the past participle must agree with the gender and number of the direct object. Such changes in word order may occur as a result of:

(a)  using a pronoun:
     Jean l'a fermée   (subject – object – verb)
(b)  using 'que':
     La porte que Jean a fermée   (object – subject – verb)
(c)  phrasing a question:
     Quelle porte est-ce que Jean a fermée?   (object – subject – verb)

To remember when to apply this rule look out for the warning signs:

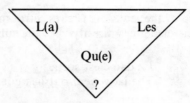

N.B.    'L(a)' and 'les' always require an agreement as may other direct
object pronouns.

Que warns of an agreement. *Check* if the preceding word is
feminine or plural.

Certain interrogative sentences, but not all, start with the object.

Reflexive verbs, which form their perfect tense with être, also
apply this rule (see Chapter 17). The reflexive pronoun is usually
the direct object of the verb.

### Exercise A

Fill in the gaps in this passage with suitable adjectives chosen from the
list below.

Les relations ＿＿＿＿＿ avec les ＿＿＿＿＿ branches de la
compagnie, l'entrée à ses ＿＿＿＿＿ resources et à l'expérience
＿＿＿＿＿ dans ＿＿＿＿＿ pays, sont à la base d'innovations
＿＿＿＿＿ qui permettent le développement d'une ＿＿＿＿＿
variété de produits.

technologiques, accumulée, autres, étroites, grande, immenses, différents

## Possessive adjectives (my, your, his, her, our, their)

Each possessive adjective has different forms to match exactly the word
it is qualifying.

|  | *masculine* | *feminine* | *plural* |
|---|---|---|---|
| my | mon | ma | mes |
| your | ton | ta | tes |
| his, her or its | son | sa | ses |
| our | notre | notre | nos |
| your | votre | votre | vos |
| their | leur | leur | leurs |

*Note* again the familiar and general forms of 'your'.

To avoid difficulties of pronunciation, 'ma', 'ta', and 'sa' are replaced
by 'mon', 'ton', and 'son' when the word that follows begins with a
vowel sound.

Examples:        mon école        ton attitude

The form of the possessive adjective is always determined by the number and gender of the word which follows. It does not show the gender of the person who owns, as it may in English.

Examples: His aunt – sa tante
Her uncle – son oncle

'Il n'aime pas sa belle-mère.'

## Demonstrative adjectives (this, that, these, those)

Like 'nouveau', 'beau' and 'vieux' there is a special form for use before masculine singular nouns beginning with a vowel sound.

| *masculine* | *feminine* | *plural* |
|---|---|---|
| ce (cet) | cette | ces |

Examples: Ce monsieur est gentil
Cette femme est ravissante
Cet homme est dangéreux

To show the difference between 'this' and 'that', 'these' and 'those', the suffixes '-ci' and '-là' are added.

Example: Je préfère cette voiture-ci à cette voiture-là
I prefer this car to that car

## Exercise B

Because adjectives never change their spelling in English it is a common mistake to forget to make an agreement change in French. Read the following passage carefully and correct the missed or wrong agreements.

Mettez-vous au volant d'un 'Lynx' 209. Il aime les situations les plus défavorable. Son pneus vous donnent la meilleur adhérence dans toute les conditions. Sa systèmes de suspension novateur, vantée continuellement, ajouté à une traction intégraux, permanent, perfectionnés, en sont la preuve.

# 14
# Adverbs and prepositions

## Adverbs

Adverbs do for verbs what adjectives do for nouns – they describe
them. They add something to the verb. They are related to adjectives
in that the majority are formed by adding '-ment' to the feminine form
of the adjective. The suffix '-ment' corresponds to '-ly' in English.
Unlike adjectives, the spelling of adverbs never varies.

| adjective (m) | adjective(f) | adverb |
|---|---|---|
| heureux | heureuse | heureusement |
| happy | happy | happily |

As you might expect, not every adverb follows this simple rule, but the
number of exceptions is not so large as those found among adjectives.
Exceptions:
1  Adjectives ending in a vowel do not add 'e' before adding '-ment'
   to become adverbs.
   e.g.    poli            –       poliment        (politely)
2  Adjectives ending in '-ent' and '-ant' change to '-emment' and
   '-amment' respectively to become adverbs.
   e.g.    prudent         –       prudemment    (carefully)
           courant         –       couramment    (fluently)
   N.B. Both adverb endings have the same pronunciation.
3  A few adverbs emphasize the feminine ending '-e' with an acute
   accent when forming the adverb.
   e.g.    aveugle         –       aveuglément    (blindly)

## Some common adverbs

The most common adverbs are often short words which do not end in
'-ment'.

*Adverbs of quantity*

| beaucoup | tant | peu | trop |
|----------|------|-----|------|
| a lot | so much | a little | too much |

Example:  Elle parle beaucoup et travaille peu

*Adverbs of place*

| en bas | en haut | quelque part |
|--------|---------|--------------|
| downstairs | upstairs | somewhere |
| nulle part | ailleurs | partout |
| nowhere | elsewhere | everywhere |

Example:  J'ai cherché partout mais je ne l'ai pas trouvé.
Ça doit être ailleurs.

*Adverbs of time*

| après | bientôt | d'abord | toujours |
|-------|---------|---------|----------|
| after | soon | at first | always |
| puis | ensuite | enfin | quelquefois |
| then | next | at last | sometimes |

'Métro, boulot, dodo.
D'abord on prend le train.
Puis on va au travail.
Enfin on se couche.'

## Comparative of adverbs and adjectives – more or less

Both adverbs and adjectives can be modified by adding 'plus' (more) or 'moins' (less).

e.g.
|  |  |
|---|---|
| extraordinare | plus extraordinaire |
| extraordinary | more extraordinary |
| fantastique | moins fantastique |
| fantastic | less fantastic |
| lentement | plus lentement |
| slowly | more slowly |
| vite | moins vite |
| quickly | less quickly |

## Superlative of adverbs and adjectives – the most

By adding 'le' to the comparative of adverbs and either 'le', 'la' or 'les' to the comparative of adjectives, the superlative is formed.

Example:    On monte le plus lentement au sommet de la Tour Eiffel, mais la vue du haut est la plus spectaculaire de tout Paris.
You climb most slowly to the top of the Eiffel Tower, but the view from the top is the most spectacular of all Paris.

*Special cases*
In English we often use separate words ending in '-er' and '-est' to express comparative and superlative forms.
e.g.   big      bigger      biggest
Only three French adjectives and their corresponding adverbs do something similar to this.

| *adjectives* |  | *adverbs* |  |
|---|---|---|---|
| bon | (good) | bien | (well) |
| meilleur | (better) | mieux | (better) |
| le meilleur | (best) | le mieux | (best) |
| mauvais | (bad) | mal | (badly) |
| pire | (worse) | pis | (worse) |
| le pire | (worst) | le pis | (worst) |
| petit | (small) | peu | (little) |
| moindre | (less) | moins | (less) |
| le moindre | (least) | le moins | (least) |

Notice that the comparative and superlative of both adjectives and adverbs have the same translation in English. To decide which form to use, remember that the adjective is longer than the adverb, just as the word 'adjective' has more letters than the word 'adverb'.

e.g.        C'est le meilleur [*adjective*] joueur de l'équipe.
Il joue mieux [*adverb*] que tous les autres.

There are no alternatives to meilleur and mieux, whereas the forms plus mauvais and plus petit do exist. The special forms are used for abstract words only, e.g. Je n'ai pas la moindre idée.

**Exercise A**

1

Here are three young people with their marks for a recent maths test. Compare them in as many ways as possible, e.g. Bernard est plus grand que Nathalie mais il est moins intelligent qu'elle.

2 Adverbs can often be expressed by an adverbial phrase.
e.g. amoureusement – lovingly *or* avec amour – with love

Juliette telephones Romeo asking him about his love for her. Repeat Romeo's protestations using adverbs instead of the adverbial phrases.

| | |
|---|---|
| Juliette: | Comment est-ce que tu m'aimes? |
| Romeo: | Avec passion, folie, tendresse, dévotion et désespoir. |
| Juliette: | Pour combien de temps m'aimeras-tu? |
| Romeo: | Pour l'éternité, jusqu'à la fin du temps. |
| Juliette: | Tu peux venir me voir? |
| Romeo: | Je regrette. J'ai mal à la jambe, je marche avec difficulté, et en plus il pleut. |

## Prepositions

Prepositions are short words, often denoting place or position, whose correct use causes problems to foreign language learners generally.

In English they can be used to modify verbs which in French will be expressed by a completely different verb.

| | | | | | |
|---|---|---|---|---|---|
| e.g. | go | – aller | | go **up** | – monter |
| | go **down** | – descendre | | go **in** | – entrer |
| | go **out** | – sortir | | go **off** | – partir |
| | go **through across** | – traverser | | go **back** | – retourner |

Some common prepositions:

| | | | | |
|---|---|---|---|---|
| sur | – on | | par | – through |
| sous | – under | | à côté de | – beside |
| derrière | – behind | | jusqu'à | – until |
| devant | – in front | | travers | – across |
| sans | – without | | après | – after |
| avec | – with | | avant | – before |

The two most common and most important prepositions are 'à' and 'de'. These combine with the definite article to form separate words:

| | | |
|---|---|---|
| (à + le) au | – | to the |
| (à + les) aux | – | to the |
| (de + le) du | – | of the |
| (de + les) des | – | of the |

In the other forms the two words remain separate, e.g. 'à la,' 'de l''.

## Verbs and prepositions

The following verbs include prepositions in their make up. Be careful when you use them.

| | | | |
|---|---|---|---|
| attendre | – to wait for | chercher | – to look for |
| demander | – to ask for | payer | – to pay for |
| écouter | – to listen to | regarder | – to look at |

e.g.        J'attends le bus

Conversely there are some French verbs which always require a preposition (usually à or de) when used with an accompanying noun:

| se souvenir de | – to remember | s'approcher de | – to approach |
|---|---|---|---|
| sortir de | – to leave | entrer dans | – to enter |
| obéir à | – to obey | répondre à | – to answer |

e.g.      Le voleur est sorti de l'appartement quand il a vu le propriétaire entrer dans l'immeuble.

## Exercise B

1    Pick out the prepositions in this passage. What happens?

Jojo sort de son trou. Il jette un coup d'oeil vers la table. Avec précaution il s'avance dans la salle et s'approche de la table sous laquelle se trouve un petit morceau de fromage. Vite il le saisit, mais, à ce moment, Tom s'élance de derrière la porte et la chasse commence.

2    Now tell in French the rest of the story.

Jerry runs towards his hole but Tom blocks his way. Tom chases Jerry three times around the table. Jerry runs under the sofa, along the radiator on to the table, behind a chair and, at last, finds his hole again.

*vocabulary*

| court | runs |
|---|---|
| barre le chemin | blocks the way |
| chasse | chases |
| retrouve | finds again |
| autour de | around |
| le long de | along |

## Prepositions and infinitives

When two verbs with the same subject come together in a sentence, the second one is an infinitive.

Example:    Je veux aller au cinéma, mais je ne peux pas sortir ce soir.

The verbs are sometimes found, as in the example, with nothing to separate them, sometimes with a preposition (usually de or à) between them. It is difficult to give rules whether to separate or not. The first verb determines the construction.

Here are some guidelines to help.

*Verbs which take no preposition*

| (a) | vouloir | – to wish/want | pouvoir | – to be able |
|---|---|---|---|---|
| | devoir | – to have to/must | aller | – to go |

| faire | – | to do/make | oser | – | to dare |
|-------|---|------------|------|---|---------|
| aimer | – | to like | savoir | – | to know (how to) |
| espérer | – | to hope | croire | – | to believe |
| il faut | – | it is necessary | | | |

(b)  verbs of seeing and hearing:

| voir | – | to see | regarder | – | to look at |
|------|---|--------|----------|---|-----------|
| entendre | – | to hear | écouter | – | to listen to |

*Verbs which require 'à'*

(a)  verbs of starting:

commencer à  –  to begin          se mettre à  –  to start

(b)  verbs indicating spending time:

| passer son temps à | – | to spend time |
|--------------------|---|---------------|
| perdre son temps à | – | to waste time |
| s'amuser à | – | to enjoy |

(c)  verbs of continuing and succeeding:

continuer à – to continue          réussir à – to succeed

---

**Bulletin: Michel Deblaise**
**Mathématiques:** Michel ne réussira jamais à comprendre s'il continue à perdre son temps à regarder par la fenêtre.

---

*Verbs which require 'de'*

(a)  verbs which take indirect, personal objects (i.e. lui *not* le or la, leur *not* les)

| conseiller | – | to advise | défendre | – | to forbid |
|------------|---|-----------|----------|---|-----------|
| demander | – | to ask | dire | – | to say/tell |
| ordonner | – | to order | permettre | – | to allow |
| promettre | – | to promise | | | |

Example:        Elle lui a demandé de sortir

(b)  most verbs formed by être and an adjective

| être content | – | to be pleased | être heureux | – | to be happy |
|--------------|---|---------------|--------------|---|-------------|
| être désolé | – | to be sorry | être triste | – | to be sad |

Example: Elle était triste de le voir quitter l'immeuble

(c)  these common verbs

| | | | | |
|---|---|---|---|---|
| cesser | – | to cease/finish | finir | – | to finish |
| décider | – | to decide | essayer | – | to try |
| regretter | – | to be sorry | | |

> Example:  Mais, elle avait décidé de cesser de l'aimer – si possible

N.B. Prepositions govern infinitives in French, not present participles as often happens in English. In other words, a present participle will usually follow a preposition in English, but an infinitive will follow in French. Always check your written work carefully for this point.

> Example:  Lui, les mains dans le poche, il a traversé la rue sans **tourner** la tête et a commencé à **siffler**.
> With his hands in his pockets, he crossed the street without **looking** back and began **whistling**

## Exercise C

1  Pick out the prepositions in the following passage.

Nous décollons à Dubai et montons sans secousse jusqu'à 10,000 mètres. Dehors, l'air passe sur l'avion à une vitesse incroyable. A 04h 15, l'aube se lève. Le soleil levant est derrière nous. Au-dessus des Alpes nous faisons face à un orage. Un éclair illumine les nuages tout près de l'avion, mais le danger passe et bientôt le soleil retourne. La Tamise apparaît au-dessous de nous. A 09h 25 nous nous approchons de Heathrow où nous devons atterrir à 09h 30. L'avion commence à descendre et nous nous préparons à débarquer sans penser aux dangers de la nuit.

2  Now translate the passage.

# 15
# Verbs 1: present, interrogation, negation, future, past historic

The heart of any sentence is the verb. Without it no sentence is complete. The French verbal system is complicated and there are many irregular forms, but it is logical and there are ground rules to help you master it. Regular verbs are those which obey rules (les règles), irregular verbs those that deviate in some way from them. Many commonly used verbs are irregular. The reason for this is not hard to find. An object which is handled frequently will give evidence of its use by changing its appearance. For example, two brand new books are placed in a library, one is a learned treatise, the other a popular novel. The former retains its pristine condition because it lacks popular appeal and usage; the latter soon becomes dog-eared from use, with pages torn or missing. In short, it becomes considerably changed through the use people have made of it.

Language changes also. New words are introduced, others drop in and out of fashion. Before the advent of printing in the late fifteenth century, language was even more fluid. Once the written word could be seen by large numbers of people, the language began to be codified, grammatical rules were established and the form of common, irregular verbs for example was stabilized.

Verbs denote actions. These can take place at different times – or in different tenses. This chapter deals with three tenses called simple tenses, not necessarily because they are easy, but because each tense consists of one word.

Regular verbs are divided into three groups or conjugations, recognizable by the endings of the infinitive. They are:

| | | | | |
|---|---|---|---|---|
| 1st conjugation: | 'er' | verbs | e.g. | porter (to wear/carry) |
| 2nd conjugation: | 'ir' | verbs | e.g. | finir (to finish) |
| 3rd conjugation: | 're' | verbs | e.g. | vendre (to sell) |

There is only one completely irregular verb which ends in 'er' – aller (to go). Many irregular verbs end in 'oir'.

## Present tense

This tense tells you of actions taking place now, at this moment. Regular verbs form their present tense by substituting the last two letters of the infinitive for an ending which varies according to the subject.

| *'er' verbs (e.g. porter)* | | | *'ir' verbs (e.g. finir)* | |
|---|---|---|---|---|
| *je* | -e | (porte) | -is | (finis) |
| *tu* | -es | (portes) | -is | (finis) |
| *il/elle* | -e | (porte) | -it | (finit) |
| *nous* | -ons | (portons) | -issons | (finissons) |
| *vous* | -ez | (portez) | -issez | (finissez) |
| *ils/elles* | -ent | (portent) | -issent | (finissent) |

| *'re' verbs (e.g. vendre)* | | |
|---|---|---|
| *je* | -s | (vends) |
| *tu* | -s | (vends) |
| *il/elle* | - | (vend) |
| *nous* | -ons | (vendons) |
| *vous* | -ez | (vendez) |
| *ils/elles* | -ent | (vendent) |

Spelling changes considerably, pronunciation not so frequently e.g.'er' verbs have five spelling changes but only three sound changes in this tense. Always check the written form carefully with the subject.

## First conjugation variations

A group of verbs in the first conjugation add a grave accent( ` ) to the 'e' before the final consonant, or else double this consonant in the first, second and third person singular and the third person plural.

All verbs in this group end 'e consonant er'.

e.g.     **mener** (to lead)     **jeter** (to throw)

The reason, once again, is a phonetic one. The accent or added consonant means that the penultimate 'e' is stressed. Without this addition, it would sound like the 'e' in the final syllable. In the examples below the irregular forms are marked with an asterisk.

| | | |
|---|---|---|
| je | mène* | jette* |
| tu | mènes* | jettes* |
| il/elle | mène* | jette* |
| nous | menons | jetons |
| vous | menez | jetez |
| ils/elles | mènent* | jettent* |

This feature reappears in the future and conditional tenses.

Another spelling change found only in 'er' verbs occurs in the first person plural. If the infinitive ends in 'ger' or 'cer' the first person plural forms end in 'geons' and 'çons'.

e.g.          nous mangeons (we eat)      nous lançons (we fling)

Phonetics again provide the reason. The letters 'g' and 'c' have different pronunciations according to the letters which follow them. They both have a soft sound when followed by 'e' or 'i' and a hard sound when followed by 'a', 'o' or 'u'.

| *soft* | | *hard* | |
|---|---|---|---|
| orange | (like 's' in leisure) | gomme | (like 'g' in gale) |
| face | (like 's' in race) | comme | (like 'k' in kitchen) |

Only in 'nous' does the ending not begin with the letter 'e', so 'ger' verbs add an 'e' to keep the sound consistent. With 'cer' verbs the addition of a cedilla ( ¸ ) ensures that the pronunciation of the 'c' is the same throughout.

This rule again comes into play in the past historic and imperfect tenses.

**Irregular verbs**

The present tense of each irregular verb has to be learned separately, but here are some pointers to help master them:

1    There are sub-groups of irregular verbs which have established their own patterns of conjugation. Here are some common examples:

| *verbs ending in* | *infinitives* |
|---|---|
| 'aître' | connaître, paraître |
| 'indre' | peindre, joindre, craindre |
| 'ir' | sortir, partir |
| 'rir' | ouvrir, offrir |
| 'uire' | conduire, construire |

2    The first person plural form (nous) always ends in 'ons', with just one exception – être (nous sommes).

3    The second person plural form (vous) always ends in 'ez', with a handful of exceptions – être (vous êtes), faire (vous faites), dire (vous dites).

4    The third person plural (ils/elles) always ends in 'ent', with the following exceptions – être (ils/elles sont), avoir (ils/elles ont), faire (ils/elles font), aller (ils/elles vont).

5    The first and second person singular (je and tu) are often spelt the same and end in 's' or 'x', the third person singular (il/elle) ends in 't'. All three persons often have the same pronunciation.

e.g.

| *voir* | *pouvoir* |
|--------|-----------|
| je vois | je peux |
| tu vois | tu peux |
| il/elle voit | il/elle peut |

6   A change in the stem of the verb sometimes occurs in the first and second person plural; in such cases the vowel sound in the third person plural reverts to the sound of the singular.

e.g.                          *devoir*

| je dois | nous **dev**ons |
|---------|-----------------|
| tu dois | vous **dev**ez |
| il/elle doit | ils/elles **doi**vent |

7   Some common 'ir' verbs behave like 'er' verbs. Common examples are ouvrir, couvrir, and cueillir.

*ouvrir*

| j'ouvre | nous ouvrons |
|---------|--------------|
| tu ouvres | vous ouvrez |
| il/elle ouvre | ils/elles ouvrent |

## Use

The present tense has only one form in French but can be expressed three ways in English – e.g. je parle:

I speak      I am speaking      I do speak

Take care not to invent an extended form in French, particularly when rendering an interrogative or negative.

Occasionally a present tense in French expresses a past tense in English.

e.g.       Il pleut depuis une heure
           It has been raining for an hour

The present tense is preferred here because, when this statement is made, it is still raining.

Look out for:       depuis   + length of time (French)
                    for      + length of time (English)

## Interrogation (asking questions)

Questions can be asked in three ways:
(a)   By tone of voice. Raise your voice at the end of the sentence to turn a statement into a question, just as you would do in English.
      e.g. Jean est à la maison?

'Mon père est en prison depuis dix ans.
Malheureusement, il est toujours là.'

(b)  By introducing the question with 'est-ce que'.
     e.g. Est-ce que Jean est à la maison?
(c)  By inversion involving a pronoun.
     e.g. Jean, est-il à la maison?

## Negation (saying 'not', etc.)

Negation involves putting 'ne' in front of the verb and a suitable form of the negative afterwards.

Here are the most common forms. The position of the verb is represented by dashes.

| | | |
|---|---|---|
| ne _____ | pas | not |
| ne _____ | point | not (more emphatic – not at all) |
| ne _____ | plus | no more/longer |
| ne _____ | jamais | never |
| ne _____ | rien | nothing |
| ne _____ | personne | nobody |
| ne _____ | aucun(e) | not one/no |

ne _____ nul(le)        not one/no
ne _____ni ... ni       neither ...nor

> Example:        Je ne fume plus les cigarettes
>                 I don't smoke cigarettes any more
>                 Moi, je n'ai jamais fumé
>                 I have never smoked

N.B.'ne _____ que' (only) behaves like a negative although it isn't one really:

> Example:        Je ne fume que les cigares
>                 I only smoke cigars

Some negatives can be used as the subject of the verb (rien, personne, aucun, nul); in this case they will precede the verb. Do not forget the 'ne'!

> Example:        Rien n'est arrivé parce que personne ne m'a vu
>                 Nothing happened because no-one saw me

## Exercise A

1   Rewrite the following passage, replacing 'nous' by 'je' and 'vous' by 'tu', making all the necessary changes.

Vous ignorez que nous sommes les premiers chimistes industriels du monde. Nous ne parlons jamais de nos recherches sur le cancer et le SIDA. Si nous remportons un succès sur le diagnostique de cette maladie, pouvez-vous continuer à rester ignorant de notre nom?

2   Rewrite the following passage changing the subject of verbs from the third person singular to the third person plural and making any necessary changes.

Il est adolescent. Il ne sait presque rien de la grande fête de Jeanne d'Arc dont il fait partie. Il porte un uniforme para-militaire et il chante des refrains guerriers. Il ne choisit pas son chemin. Il suit son chef. Il attend l'ordre, et quand il arrive à l'estrade, il hurle son slogan, 'Qui ose – gagne!'

## Future tense

In English this is expressed simply by adding 'will' or 'shall' to the verb. In French there is a separate formation. Knowing a little of the historical background to the French language will help you to remember the formation of the future tense.

French evolved from the Latin spoken by Roman soldiers during their occupation of Gaul. Their dialect was not the exact, meticulous language of classical Latin. They used short cuts whenever possible and this happened in their expression of tenses of verbs. To indicate a past tense, they used the verb 'to have' before the main verb and for the future placed it after.

These forms have evolved in modern French into the perfect and future tenses. In the perfect tenses, 'avoir' remains separated from the main verb, in the future it is fused into the infinitive to form one word.

Thus, the future tense in French is formed by using the infinitive of the verb (dropping the 'e' where necessary so that the last letter of the stem is 'r') and adding the present tense of 'avoir'. In the 'nous' and 'vous' forms the normal endings 'ons' and 'ez' are used instead of the full forms 'avons' and 'avez'. Here are the regular forms for the three conjugations:

|  | *porter* | *finir* | *vendre* |
|---|---|---|---|
| je | porterai | finirai | vendrai |
| tu | porteras | finiras | vendras |
| il/elle | portera | finira | vendra |
| nous | porterons | finirons | vendrons |
| vous | porterez | finirez | vendrez |
| ils/elles | porteront | finiront | vendront |

**Irregular stems**

All verbs, regular and irregular, end in the same way in the future. Some, but not all, irregular verbs have stems which are not the infinitive.

e.g.  être – je serai (I will be)

Here are some ways to help you remember them:

1  The stem has been shortened by squeezing out the final vowel(s):
   e.g.  courir   –   je courrai   (I will run)
          devoir   –   je devrai   (I will have to)

2  One verb has copied another:
   e.g.  avoir   –   j'aurai   (I will have)
          savoir   –   je saurai   (I will know)

          voir   –   je verrai   (I will see)
          envoyer   –   j'enverrai   (I will send)

3  A 'd' has been introduced to ease pronunciation:
   e.g.  venir   –   je viendrai   (I will come)
          vouloir   –   je voudrai   (I will wish)

4  Cueillir still thinks its an 'er' verb!
   e.g.  cueillir   –   je cueillerai   (I will gather)

5  Those 'er' verbs which added a grave accent or doubled a consonant in the present tense do the same in every person in the future tense:

| e.g. | mener | – | je mènerai | (I will lead) |
| | | | nous mènerons | (we will lead) |
| | | | ils mèneront | (they will lead) |
| | jeter | – | tu jetteras | (you will throw) |
| | | | il jettera | (he will throw) |
| | | | vous jetterez | (you will throw) |

6   Learn the first person singular form; the stem will be the same for all persons:

e.g.   faire   –   je ferai   (I will do)

Irregular futures not already mentioned:

| aller | – | j'irai | (I will go) |
| mourir | – | je mourrai | (I will die) |
| pleuvoir | – | il pleuvra | (It will rain) |
| pouvoir | – | je pourrai | (I will be able) |
| recevoir | – | je recevrai | (I will receive) |
| tenir | – | je tiendrai | (I will hold) |

The future tense can also be expressed by the verb 'aller' combined with the infinitive. This corresponds to the construction 'to be going to do' in English and expresses an immediate future action.

Example:   Il va pleurer
He is going to cry

## Use

On most occasions, when to use the future tense is obvious. Sometimes, however, the word 'will' denotes 'willingness' rather than future action. When that occurs, 'will' is expressed by using the verb 'vouloir'.

Example:   Voulez-vous vous asseoir
Will you sit down

Note also the use of the future tense in the following sentence where it translates an English present tense:

When I get home I will telephone you.
Quand j'**arriverai** chez moi, je vous téléphonerai.

This happens in expressions of time introduced by 'quand', 'lorsque' (when), dès que, aussitôt que (as soon as) when the main verb is in the future.

'Mais, c'est la logique française.'

(When you think about it, it is!)

**Exercise B**

1    Rewrite this passage using future tenses to replace the constructions aller + infinitive.

Dimanche prochain on va savoir le résultat final des élections législatives. Est-ce que le parti socialiste va obtenir a majorité absolue de sièges, ou est-ce que la droite va remporter la victoire? Quelle va être la situation vis-à-vis le Président? Va-t-il devoir essayer de constituer une coalition ou une sorte d'union nationale? Tout va dépendre sur le système compliqué de voter en France. Ce qui est certain, c'est que les sondages vont se tromper encore une fois.

2    Translate the passage into English.

*vocabulary*

| | |
|---|---|
| sièges (m) | seats |
| sondages (m) | opinion polls |
| vis-à-vis | with regard to |
| se tromper | to make a mistake |

## Past historic tense

The past historic is a tense found only in the written form. It has evolved from the classical Latin past tense. Its equivalent in speech is the perfect tense; this is much more widely used and is written as well as spoken.

It must be used, for example, when writing letters in the past tense. The past historic is limited to narrating events, usually in works of literature. You will read it also in newspapers. It is a tense you need to recognize more often than use.

## Formation

There are two different sets of endings which, as in the present tense, replace the last two letters of the infinitive, for all regular verbs:

|          | *'er' verbs*<br>*e.g. porter* | *'ir' verbs*<br>*e.g. finir* | *'re' verbs*<br>*e.g. vendre* |
|----------|----------|----------|----------|
| je       | portai   | finis    | vendis   |
| tu       | portas   | finis    | vendis   |
| il/elle  | porta    | finit    | vendit   |
| nous     | portâmes | finîmes  | vendîmes |
| vous     | portâtes | finîtes  | vendîtes |
| ils/elles| portèrent| finirent | vendirent|

The endings of the first three persons of 'er' verbs are the same as those found in the future tense. To avoid confusion, remember that all future forms will feature an 'r' before the ending. This will prevent you making a mistake in the majority of 'er' verbs.

Verbs that end in the infinitive '–ger' and '–cer' again take an extra 'e' and cedilla respectively as they did in the present tense (see p. 92). The additions are required in all persons except the last.

N.B.    'Aller' forms its past historic tense normally. 'ir' verbs are spelt the same way in the first three persons in the past historic and present tenses.

## Irregular verbs

The formation of the past historic of irregular verbs is not so complicated as that of the present tense, in that there are only three sets of endings.
    Many irregular verbs use the same endings as 'ir' and 're' verbs:

| e.g. | faire    | – | je fis      | (I made) |
|------|----------|---|-------------|----------|
|      | dire     | – | je dis      | (I said) |
|      | s'asseoir| – | je m'assis  | (I sat)  |

Most 'oir' verbs take a set of endings similar to those found in 'ir' verbs except that the 'i' is replaced by 'u'. An example is 'avoir':

| j'eus   (I had) | nous eûmes       |
|-----------------|------------------|
| tu eus          | vous eûtes       |
| il/elle eut     | ils/elles eurent |

Here is a list of some common irregular verbs. Note how the first person past historic is similar to the past participle (pronunciation is identical):

| *infinitive* | | *past historic* | | *past participle* |
|---|---|---|---|---|
| devoir | – | je dus | (I had to) | dû |
| pouvoir | – | je pus | (I was able) | pu |
| recevoir | – | je reçus | (I received) | reçu |
| vouloir | – | je voulus | (I wished) | voulu |
| connaître | – | je connus | (I knew) | connu |
| courir | – | je courus | (I ran) | couru |
| falloir | – | il fallut | (it was necessary) | fallu |

*but*

| être | – | je fus | (I was) | été |
|---|---|---|---|---|
| voir | – | je vis | (I saw) | vu |

There is a small group of irregulars clustered around the verbs 'venir' and 'tenir', which are different again in the past historic:

*venir*

| je vins | (I came) | nous vînmes |
|---|---|---|
| tu vins | | vous vîntes |
| il/elle vint | | ils/elles vinrent |

Similar verbs are:
revenir (to come back), devenir (to become), appartenir (to belong), retenir (to retain)

## Use

The tense is used to depict single, completed events in the past tense in a simple, direct manner.

Example:          César: Il vint, il vit, il conquit.

## Exercise C

1   Rewrite the following story putting the verbs from the perfect tense into the past historic.

En 1661, on a envoyé un prisonnier, jeune, beau, noble, au Château de l'Ile Marguerite, une île dans la Méditerranée. Le prisonnier portait un masque de fer qu'il gardait toujours au visage. Il est resté sur l'île 29 ans. En 1690, le gouverneur de la Bastille, Saint Mars, l'a conduit à Paris.

Un jour le prisonnier mystérieux a écrit avec un couteau sur une assiette qu'il a jetée par la fenêtre à un bateau tout près de la tour. Un pêcheur sur le bateau a pris l'assiette et l'a montrée au gouverneur. Le pêcheur, heuresement, ne savait pas lire, et Sainte Mars l'a laissé partir.

En 1703 l'homme au masque de fer est mort et on l'a enterré à Saint Paul. L'identité de ce prisonnier important, sans doute un noble, reste un mystère.

2   Answer these questions:
(a)   Where was the prisoner first sent?
(b)   How long did he stay there?
(c)   Where was his second prison?
(d)   How did the man in the mask get a message out of prison?
(e)   Why was the fisherman lucky?

*(Voltaire tells this story in his history 'Le Siècle de Louis XIV'.)*

# 16
# Verbs 2: imperfect, conditional

## Imperfect tense

This common past tense is easy to form and the endings for most persons have the same pronunciation. There is only one exception to the rule governing its formation.

## Formation

The stem (the part of the verb which does not change) is that of the first person plural of the present tense, i.e. the 'nous' form minus 'ons.'

e.g.    parlons   –   parl       finissons   –   finiss
        vendons   –   vend       faisons     –   fais

The only exception to this is être, whose stem is ét.
  Verbs which end in '-ger' and '-cer' add the e or cedilla respectively in all persons of the imperfect except the first and second plural.

The endings for all verbs are the same:

|           | singular | plural |
|-----------|----------|--------|
| 1st person | -ais    | -ions  |
| 2nd person | -ais    | -iez   |
| 3rd person | -ait    | -aient |

Some verbs conjugated:

|          | parler    | manger     | finir      | être     |
|----------|-----------|------------|------------|----------|
| je       | parlais   | mangeais   | finissais  | étais    |
| tu       | parlais   | mangeais   | finissais  | étais    |
| il/elle  | parlait   | mangeait   | finissait  | était    |
| nous     | parlions  | mangions   | finissions | étions   |
| vous     | parliez   | mangiez    | finissiez  | étiez    |
| ils/elles | parlaient | mangeaient | finissaient | étaient |

## Use

The two main past tenses are the perfect and the imperfect. Understanding their titles helps toward understanding their functions. To 'perfect' is to complete, and the perfect tense describes single and completed actions. Imperfect indicates incomplete, and one use of the imperfect tense is to refer to actions which are not completed or to a state of affairs existing at some point of time in the past.

To get **RID** of the problem of wondering when to use the imperfect tense remember three specific occasions:

**R**epetition    **I**ncompletion    **D**escription    =    **RID**

### Repetition

When a past action was habitual and often repeated, the imperfect tense is used in French. In English this is expressed by putting 'used to' or 'would' in front of the verb.

Example:    Avant mon mariage, j'**allais** souvent au cinema.
I often **used to go** to the cinema before I got married.

### Incompletion

Incomplete actions are expressed by using the form 'was doing' in English and the imperfect tense in French.

Example:    Je **faisais** mes devoirs quand le téléphone a sonné.
I **was doing** my homework when the 'phone rang.

Example:    Je **nageais** de plus en plus lentement quand l' hélicoptère est arrivé.
I **was swimming** slower and slower when the helicopter arrived.

### Description

A very common use of the imperfect tense is to describe. The imperfect is used to set the scene, describe the people, surroundings, weather, etc., before the main events are related in the perfect tense.

Example:    Il **était** six heures, mais il **faisait** déjà noir. Quelques lumières **brillaient** dans les fenêtres des maisons qui **entouraient** la place.
It **was** six o'clock but already it **was getting** dark. Some lights **shone** in the windows of the houses which **surrounded** the square.

## Exercise A

Rewrite the following passage in the past tense.

Elle porte un vieux chandail. Sa jupe qui date de trois ans, laisse voir ses genoux. Elle est vêtue pour la pêche. Elle a les cheveux courts et les bras et les jambes bronzés. Quand elle sourit, ce qu'elle fait rarement, son visage s'illumine. Elle a quinze ans et demi.

Son compagnon, qui a un an de plus qu'elle, la regarde. Chaque année ils passent leurs vacances d'été ensemble. Enfants, ils jouent heureusement ensemble, mais cette année l'adolescence les sépare.

*(Read more of this story and the pangs of adolescence in 'Le Blé en Herbe' by Colette.)*

## Conditional tense

### Formation

The conditional tense is linked to the imperfect in that they both have the same set of endings. The stem of the conditional is the same as that of the future tense and always ends in 'r'. This feature allows one to distinguish between the conditional and the imperfect.

e.g.          *conditional*    *imperfect*
              Je parlerais      Je parlais

Verbs which added a grave accent (mener) or doubled a consonant (jeter) in the future, do so also in the conditional:

|          | *finir*    | *mener*    | *être*   |
|----------|------------|------------|----------|
| je       | finirais   | mènerais   | serais   |
| tu       | finirais   | mènerais   | serais   |
| il/elle  | finirait   | mènerait   | serait   |
| nous     | finirions  | mènerions  | serions  |
| vous     | finiriez   | mèneriez   | seriez   |
| ils/elles| finiraient | mèneraient | seraient |

### Use

The conditional is sometimes known as the 'future in the past'. This seems a contradiction in terms but means that it is the form used when a verb in the future tense is expressed in reported or indirect speech.

'Je gagnerai au troisième round.'

Il a dit qu'il **gagnerait** au troisième round.
He said he **would win** in the third round.

The conditional tense is expressed in English by using the words 'would' or 'should' in front of the verb.

The most common and useful shopping term uses the conditional of vouloir:

je voudrais  –  I would like

The conditional tense is also used in sentences involving conditions. In English look out for the word 'if', in French for 'si'.

Example:     mais s'il parlait moins, il **aurait** plus de souffle
             but if he spoke less, he **would have** more breath

Remember this use by applying this formula:
     si + imperfect        : conditional

Change the tense of the first verb of the equation and the second tense changes also.

si + present          :   future

Example:          Si je le frappe, il tombera
                  If I hit him, he will fall down

si + pluperfect  :   conditional perfect (see pp. 112–13)

'S'il avait su ce qui allait arriver, il ne serait jamais entré dans le ring.'

## Exercise B

1   Write the following passage in reported (indirect) speech. Begin:
    'Le Président a dit que ...'

—L'Europe sera sociale ou ne sera pas. A l'Europe des marchands s'opposera celle des travailleurs. Les acquis sociaux des Français ne seront pas sacrifiés sur l'autel de la compétivité. Nous devrons entamer un dialogue social européen. Les entreprises auront un rôle important à jouer. J'attends la première réunion entre les syndiqués des filiales des multinationales, ce qui aidera à trouver une solution à notre plus grand problème – le chômage.

2   Summarize the President's feelings about:
    (a)  a united Europe
    (b)  his fears as to what might happen in France
    (c)  finding a solution to France's greatest problem.

*vocabulary*

| | |
|---|---|
| les acquis sociaux (m) | social gains |
| l'autel (m) | altar |
| entamer | to start |
| les filiales (f) | subsidiary companies |

# 17
# Verbs 3: perfect, pluperfect, future perfect, conditional perfect, past anterior

## Compound tenses

In addition to the five one-word or simple tenses met in the two preceding chapters, there are five tenses which consist of two words. These are known as compound tenses. Each simple tense is linked to a compound tense.

The most common compound tense is the perfect. Its formation is a pattern for all the other compound tenses.

## Perfect tense

### Formation

The perfect tense is formed by using the present tense of either 'avoir' or 'être' (the auxiliary verb) and adding the past participle (see pp. 78–80).

| *parler* | *dire* | *aller* |
|----------|--------|---------|
| j'ai parlé | j'ai dit | je suis allé(e) |
| tu as parlé | tu as dit | tu es allé(e) |
| il a parlé | il a dit | il est allé |
| elle a parlé | elle a dit | elle est allée |
| nous avons parlé | nous avons dit | nous sommes allé(e)s |
| vous avez parlé | vous avez dit | vous êtes allé(e)(s) |
| ils ont parlé | ils ont dit | ils sont allés |
| elles ont parlé | elles ont dit | elles sont allées |

The number of verbs which form the perfect tense with être is small, but they are often used. Remember them like this:

a) In groups:

| | |
|---|---|
| monter (to go up) | entrer (to go in) |
| descendre (to go down) | sortir (to go out) |
| partir (to leave) | aller (to go) |
| arriver (to arrive) | venir (to come) |

naître (to be born)
mourir (to die)

| | |
|---|---|
| tomber (to fall) | rentrer (to go home) |
| retourner (to return) | revenir (to come back) |
| rester (to stay) | devenir (to become) |

b)  Pictorially:

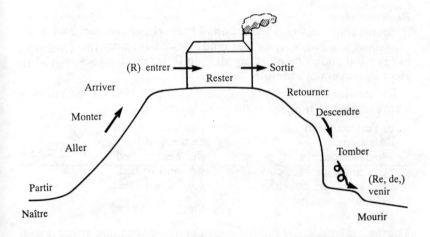

The past participle changes its spelling in order to agree with the subject in the perfect tense of these verbs (see p. 79). In other words, they behave like ordinary adjectives.

> Example:  Janine est **rentrée** a sept heures et ses amies sont **arrivées** une heure plus tard

These verbs normally take no direct object.

> Example:  Janine est entrée dans la maison
> Janine went into the house

Four of them, however, may be used with an object and when this happens they form their perfect tense with 'avoir':

monter (to go up, to put up) descendre (to go down, to take down)
sortir (to go out, to take out) rentrer (to go home, to put away)

*(Note how the meaning of the verbs has changed.)*

Example:         En arrivant à la maison, Jean a rentré son
                 vélo dans le garage, a monté l'escalier à sa
                 chambre, a descendu son sac du haut de
                 l'armoire et en a sorti un paquet de cigarettes.

                 When he arrived at the house, Jean put his
                 bike back in the garage, went upstairs to his
                 room, got his bag down from the top of the
                 wardrobe and took a packet of cigarettes out
                 of it.

*Reflexive verbs*

Reflexive verbs, in which the action of the verb is 'reflected' back upon
the subject (e.g. I hurt myself, he found himself), are much more common
in French than in English. They all form their perfect tenses with 'être'.
Here is a common example:

*se coucher*

| | |
|---|---|
| je me suis couché(e) | I went to bed |
| tu t'es couché(e) | you went to bed |
| il s'est couché | he went to bed |
| elle s'est couchée | she went to bed |
| nous nous sommes couché(e)s | we went to bed |
| vous vous êtes couché(e)(s) | you went to bed |
| ils se sont couchés | they went to bed |
| elles se sont couchées | |

The past participle is often the same number and gender as the subject
but the agreement is not direct. As with the verbs which take avoir,
the past participle agrees with the preceding direct object (see p. 79–80).
This very often is the reflexive pronoun but not always. The two verbs
'to remember' illustrate this point:

Se souvenir de quelque chose    to remind oneself of something
                                (se = direct personal object)
Se rappeler quelque chose       to recall something to oneself
                                (se = indirect personal object)

Examples:        Grand'mère s'est souvenue de sa jeunesse
                 (agreement with reflexive pronoun)
                 Elle s'est rappelé ses premiers amours
                 (no agreement with reflexive pronoun)

When using the perfect tense, the past participle comes last. Any changes
to the verb occur in the auxiliary.

e.g.     As-tu vu Pierre?   Non, je ne l'ai pas rencontré.

**Use**

It is the most common past tense and can be translated in three ways:
e.g.     J'ai mangé – I ate   I did eat   I have eaten

### Exercise A

1   Rewrite the following passages in the perfect tense. The speaker is
    a girl. Begin: 'Hier …'

    —Aujourd'hui, je me lève comme d'habitude à 6h 15 et j'attrape
    le car à 7h. On arrive au college à 8h 10 et les cours commencent
    cinq minutes plus tard. Le matin j'ai biologie, histoire, français et
    maths. Je mange au self, mais je n'ai que cinquante minutes pour
    le déjeuner. A 17h je retrouve le car pour rentrer à la maison à
    18h. Les devoirs durent deux heures et demie. Je ne regarde pas la
    télé, il n'y a pas le temps. Je monte à ma chambre à 21h 30, je mets
    un disque puis je me couche.

2   "A l'école on vous bourre le crâne," dit Katrine. Un principal de
    collège remarque que "les élèves sont stressés. Il y a toujours une
    foule à l'infirmerie."

    Il paraît que, en France, on a oublié le précepte de Montaigne,
    "Mieux vaut une tête bien faite, qu'une tête bien pleine."

    Qu'en pensez-vous? Discutez avec un(e) ami(e).

## Other compound tenses

There are four other tenses formed like the perfect. The rules of
agreement still apply. The only change occurs in the tense of the auxiliary
verb. Here are the formations:

present of auxiliary + past participle     = perfect
imperfect of auxiliary + past participle   = pluperfect
future of auxiliary + past participle      = future perfect
conditional of auxiliary + past participle = conditional perfect
past historic of auxiliary + past participle = past anterior

### Pluperfect tense

|         *parler* |          *aller* |
| --- | --- |
| j'avais parlé (I had spoken) | j'étais allé(e) (I had gone) |
| tu avais parlé | tu étais allé(e) |
| il avait parlé | il était allé |
| elle avait parlé | elle était allée |

| | |
|---|---|
| nous avions parlé | nous étions allé(e)s |
| vous aviez parlé | vous étiez allé(e)(s) |
| ils avaient parlé | ils étaient allés |
| elles avaient parlé | elles étaient allées |

The pluperfect always translates 'had done'.

Example:     Quand il **avait fini** son dîner, il est sorti
             When he **had finished** his dinner, he went out

**Future perfect**

| *finir* | *partir* |
|---|---|
| j'aurai fini | je serai parti(e) |
| (I will have finished) | (I will have left) |
| tu auras fini | tu seras parti(e) |
| il aura fini | il sera parti |
| elle aura fini | elle sera partie |
| nous aurons fini | nous serons parti(e)s |
| vous aurez fini | vous serez parti(e)(s) |
| ils auront fini | ils seront partis |
| elles auront fini | elles seront parties |

The future perfect translates '**will have** done'.

Example:     Quand nous arriverons à Nice, nous **aurons fait** 5,000 kilomètres
             When we get to Nice we **will have done** 5,000 kilometres

Watch out for the use of the future perfect in sentences using 'when' (quand, lorsque) or 'as soon as' (dès que, aussitôt que) when the main verb is in the future tense.

Example:     Aussitôt qu'il **aura fini** son dîner, il sortira.
             As soon as he **has finished** his dinner, he will go out.

Compare this with the use of the future to translate an English present tense mentioned on p. 97.

**Conditional perfect**

| *vendre* | *se lever* |
|---|---|
| j'aurais vendu | je me serais levé(e) |
| (I would have sold) | (I would have got up) |
| tu aurais vendu | tu te serais levé(e) |

| | |
|---|---|
| il aurait vendu | il se serait levé |
| elle aurait vendu | elle se serait levée |
| nous aurions vendu | nous nous serions levé(e)s |
| vous auriez vendu | vous vous seriez levé(e)(s) |
| ils auraient vendu | ils se seraient levés |
| elles auraient vendu | elles se seraient levées |

The conditional perfect translates '**would have/should have** done'.

| Example: | Elle **aurait parlé** plus tôt si elle l'avait reconnu |
|---|---|
| | She **would have spoken** earlier if she had recognized him |

Besides being found in conditional sentences like this, the conditional perfect is also required after 'quand', 'dès que' and 'aussitôt que' when the main verb is in the conditional tense.

| Example: | Il a dit que, quand il **aurait fini** son dîner, il sortirait. |
|---|---|
| | He said that, when he **had finished** his dinner, he would go out. |
| | Encore la logique française! |

Note the use of the three common auxiliary verbs 'vouloir', 'pouvoir' and 'devoir' in the conditional perfect tense.

| Examples: | Tu connais la chanson 'J'aurais pu danser toute la nuit'? |
|---|---|
| | Do you know the song 'I could have danced all night'? |
| | J'aurais voulu assister au spectacle |
| | I would like to have been to the show |
| | Tu aurais dû voir le film |
| | You ought to have seen the film |

**Past anterior**

| *faire* | *venir* |
|---|---|
| j'eus fait (I had done) | je fus venu(e) (I had come) |
| tu eus fait | tu fus venu(e) |
| il eut fait | il fut venu |
| elle eut fait | elle fut venue |
| nous eûmes fait | nous fûmes venu(e)s |
| vous eûtes fait | vous fûtes venu(e)(s) |
| ils eurent fait | ils furent venus |
| elles eurent fait | elles furent venues |

The past anterior is a rarely used tense. It translates '**had** done'. It is only found in a written form after 'quand', 'lorsque', 'dès que', 'aussitôt que', 'à peine que' or other conjunctions introducing a time clause, when the main verb is in the past historic.

Example:   A peine **fut-il sorti** que le téléphone sonna
Hardly **had he left** than the 'phone rang

## Exercise B

1   Complete the following passage by filling in the gaps with one of the verbs listed below the text.
   (The Managing Director is addressing his management team.)

'Vous serez plus motivés quand vous _____ un stage des arts martiaux,' dit le chef. Il _____ récemment un livre americain qui _____ ce nouveau méthode d'entraînement. 'J' _____ moi-meme apprendre le kendo. C'est trop tard pour moi, mais pas pour vous.' Les cadres ne dirent rien, mais quand le P D G _____, ils se regardèrent avec horreur.

avait lu    fut sorti    expliquait    aurez suivi    aurais voulu

2   Translate
   (a)  'You would have been more motivated if you had followed a martial arts course.'
   (b)  'I had wanted to learn Kendo.'
   (c)  When he had read the book, he left.

# 18
# Verbs 4: present participle, infinitive, imperative

## Present participle

Present participles are used far more frequently in English than in French. In English they are recognized by the suffix 'ing', in French they end in 'ant', e.g. walking (marchant).

The stem of the present participle in French is the same as that of the imperfect tense:

| e.g. | finir | – finissant |
|---|---|---|
| | vendre | – vendant |
| | manger | – mangeant |

There are three exceptions:

| | être | – étant |
|---|---|---|
| | avoir | – ayant |
| | savoir | – sachant |

Whereas in English a present participle is often used to form an alternative version of a particular tense, this is never the case in French.

| Example: | I was **watching** TV |
|---|---|
| *but* | Je regardais la télé |

The present participle is used to express one action going on at the same time as another.

| Example: | **Ecrivant** furieusement, elle a achevé la lettre |
|---|---|
| | **Writing** furiously, she finished the letter |

Used as a verb, the present participle does not change its spelling. Like the past participle, it can be used also as an adjective, in which case it behaves like one as far as agreement is concerned.

| | |
|---|---|
| Examples: | Les feuilles tombant de l'arbre (verb) |
| | The leaves falling from the tree |
| | |
| | Les feuilles tombantes (adjective) |
| | The falling leaves |

A common use of the present participle occurs after the preposition 'en', to translate 'on', 'by', 'while', 'from', or 'through' doing:

| | |
|---|---|
| Examples: | En entendant le téléphone, Jean s'est levé de son fauteuil |
| | On hearing the telephone, John got up from his armchair |
| | |
| | En téléphonant, belle-maman l'a réveillé |
| | By telephoning, mother-in-law woke him up |
| | |
| | En parlant à sa belle-mère, il a baîllé plusieurs fois |
| | While speaking to his mother-in-law, he yawned several times |

## Infinitives

Infinitives often take over the role of present participles in French. With the exception of 'en', every other preposition in French, when followed by a verb, is followed by an infinitive.

| | |
|---|---|
| Examples: | Sans **faire** de bruit, Jean a ramassé le téléphone |
| | Without **making** a noise, John picked up the telephone |
| | |
| | Il a réussi à **regagner** son fauteuil |
| | He succeeded in **getting back** to his chair again |
| | |
| | Belle-maman a continué à **parler** |
| | Mother-in-law carried on **talking** |
| | |
| | Jean a essayé de **se rendormir** |
| | John tried **going back to sleep again** |

Be particularly aware of the construction with the preposition 'après':

Example:        **Après avoir passé** 20 minutes au telephone,
belle-maman a enfin raccroché
**After spending** 20 minutes on the 'phone,
mother-in-law finally hung up

Infinitives are usually translated with the word 'to' in front:

Example:        Il a essayé de se rendormir
He tried **to** go back to sleep again

Whenever two verbs occur together in French with the same subject, the second is an infinitive. Remember that they may be separated by a preposition (see pp. 86–9).

## Exercise A

1  Read the following passage and answer the questions below.

L'environnement ne peut plus rester le domaine des hommes de science. Les politiques sont réunis pour discuter des moyens de protéger la couche d'ozone qui nous entoure. Ayant peur que l'avenir de la politique ne soit lié à celui du climat, les chefs des gouvernements essaient de nous persuader qu'ils s'intéressent vivement aux problèmes de l'environnement, en disant, par exemple, qu'il faut limiter la consommation des chlorofluorocarbones attaquant l'ozone.

    Les pays du tiers monde sont sceptiques, affirmant que les pays industrialisés sont en train de détruire l'ozone, donc ce sont eux qui doivent payer.

(a) How many infinitives are there in the passage?
(b) How many present participles?
(c) How many of the infinitives can be translated by English present participles?
(d) How many infinitives occur after prepositions?
(e) How many infinitives are connected with verbs having the same subject?

2   Tous les pays sont d'accord pour protéger la nature, mais comment? Vous avez une opinion?

## Imperatives

Using a verb in the imperative means using it to give an order. This is done by employing three forms of the present tense taken from the 'tu', 'nous' and 'vous' persons, without including the subject. Here is the imperative of 'finir', for example:

| tu finis | gives | finis! | – | finish! |
| vous finissez | gives | finissez! | – | finish! |
| nous finissons | gives | finissons! | – | let's finish! |

The second person singular form is used for addressing a friend, a member of the family or a child, etc.

There is a small spelling change in the singular imperative of 'er' verbs; the final 's' is omitted.

e.g.        André, mange tes choux!

There are a few irregular forms; here are the most common:

| *être* | *avoir* | *savoir* |
| sois | aie | sache |
| soyez | ayez | sachez |
| soyons | ayons | sachons |

Object pronouns used with affirmative commands come after the verb and are linked to it by hyphens (see p. 69).

e.g.        Tu as la photo? Donne-la-moi, s'il te plaît

If the command is in the negative, the pronouns return to their normal place in front of the verb.

e.g.        Ne la montre pas à Papa!

This rule explains the position of pronouns in reflexive verbs used in the imperative.

Examples:          Asseyez-vous!
                   Sit down!

                   Ne vous dépêchez pas!
                   Don't rush!

## Spelling differences between infinitives, past participles and imperatives of 'er' verbs

The endings 'er', 'é' and 'ez' have the same pronunciation. A common spelling mistake is to mix them up. Always check these endings carefully. Their contexts should tell you which is the correct form:

'er' (infinitive) follows a preposition or another verb.
'é' (past participle) follows 'avoir' or 'être'.
'ez' imperative or with subject 'vous'.

Examples:          'Vous ne voulez pas manger?'
                   'Nous avons déjà mangé.'
                   'Oui du chocolat. Ne mangez pas trop de chocolat!'

## Exercise B

1   Rewrite this passage changing from the second person plural to the second person singular form.

   Imaginez que vous êtes chez nous. Découvrez nos plages! Allongez-vous sur notre sable! Mettez les pieds dans l'eau et nagez dans la mer transparente de nos baies! Goûtez notre cuisine incomparable, mangez les fruits de mer et buvez le vin de la région!

   Où est le passé? Cherchez-le dans nos villages! Et l'avenir? Trouvez-le dans nos villes! Cachez-vous dans le sein de la nature! Venez vite et amusez-vous bien! Dépêchez-vous, les vacances vous attendent.

2   After his holiday, your friend gives you some advice. Translate his remarks.

   Don't eat the sea food! Don't drink the local wines! The past? Don't look for it in the villages! Don't hide yourself in the bosom of nature, but do go there and enjoy yourself!

# 19
# Verbs 5: passive, subjunctive

## Passive voice

When a verb has a subject and a different object, it is said to be used in the active voice.

e.g.      The boy ate an apple.

If, however, the subject and the object are the same, i.e. the action of the verb is reflected back upon the subject, the verb is said to be used in the passive.

e.g.      The apple was eaten

In English we express the passive by using the verb 'to be' and a past participle. There are just as many tenses of the passive as there are of the active voice.

e.g.      The apple is eaten      (present)
            The apple will be eaten      (future)
            The apple had been eaten      (pluperfect)

## Use

The passive is used more frequently in English than in French where often a more active way of expressing the idea is preferred. The passive construction is often formal and impersonal. Can this tell us something about the two nations?

There are three ways of expressing the passive in French.

*1 Using être and the past participle*
This is a direct translation of the English. Remember that the past participle, coming after some form of 'être', always agrees with the subject.

|  |  |
|---|---|
| Example: | Les actions du Président ont été approuvées par 56% de la population<br>The President's actions have been approved by 56% of the population |

*2 Using a reflexive verb*
Some reflexive verbs are always translated by a passive.

| e.g. | s'appeler | – | to be called |
|---|---|---|---|
|  | se trouver | – | to be found |
|  | s'intéresser à | – | to be interested in |

Example:          Ses supporters les plus fanatiques **se trouvent** parmi les membres de la classe ouvrière
His most enthusiastic supporters **are found** among the members of the working class

Others can be made reflexive in order to translate a passive.

e.g.        se vendre        –        to be sold

Only use this passive construction if you are confident it is correct.

*3   Using the verb in the active with the subject 'on'*
'On' is a most useful pronoun with no specific translation. It can be used to denote 'one', 'you', 'they' and often 'we' (see p. 67).

Example:          Qu'est-ce qu'on dira de lui l'année prochaine?
What will be said of him next year?

There are certain verbs whose passives can only be formed this way. They are verbs which take indirect, personal objects.
e.g.        donner        –        to give (to someone)

montrer        –        to show (to someone)
offrir          –        to offer (to someone)

Example:          **On a montré** au Président l'approbation de la nation pour ses actions
The President **was shown** the nation's approval of his actions

Remember also these two important verbs which take a similar construction.

dire            –        to say
demander        –        to ask

**Exercise A**

Translate the following passage into English noting the number of passives.

Le nombre de sinistres informatiques augmente d'année en année. Des chiffres alarmants de plus de 100 par jour ont été révélés par une enquête récente. Il y a 10 ans, seules l'administration et la gestion d'une entreprise étaient informatisées. Aujourd'hui on met sur disquette toutes les activités essentielles. Le coeur d'une entreprise, son information, se trouve dans les ordinateurs. Les guerres commerciales ne se gagneront plus qu'en assurant la sécurité de cette information.

Quelquefois la sécurité est minimale – les disquettes sont rangées dans un placard dont tout le monde sait où est la clef. La vraie menace, cependant, l'intervention humaine, est souvent ignorée. Beaucoup de ces criminels se trouvent dans l'entreprise elle-même.

On peut introduire un virus qui se développe de la même manière que certaines maladies physiques. La plupart des organismes financiers français ont été touchés par la fraude automatique. En Amérique on a évoqué la Mafia et on suppose que le Krach d'octobre '87 a été provoqué par une attaque (un virus peut-être) du système informatique de Wall Street.

*vocabulary*

| | |
|---|---|
| sinistres (m) informatiques | computer crimes |
| enquête (f) | enquiry |
| gestion (f) | management |
| informatiser | put on computer records |
| virus (m) | computer virus |
| évoquer | to call to mind |

## The subjunctive

The subjunctive is a group of four tenses which are found mainly in subordinate clauses. This means that there is another verb which deals with the main event of the sentence. Subjunctive verbs are always introduced by 'que' (that).

There are four tenses – present, perfect, imperfect and pluperfect. Future actions are expressed by using the present tense. There is no future in the subjunctive!

## Formation

*Present subjunctive*
The stem of the present subjunctive is taken from the third person plural (ils) of the ordinary present tense, minus 'ent'.

| e.g. | *3rd person plural present* | | *subjunctive stem* |
|---|---|---|---|
| parler | parlent | – | parl |
| finir | finissent | – | finiss |
| vendra | vendent | – | vend |
| prendre | prennent | – | prenn |

The endings are:

| | |
|---|---|
| -e | -ions |
| -es | -iez |
| -e | -ent |

These endings apply to the vast majority of French verbs. The first and second person plural forms (nous and vous) are always the same as the imperfect. This entails with some irregular verbs a change of stem just as it does in the present indicative.

e.g.
|  | *devoir* |
|---|---|
| je doive | nous devions |
| tu doives | vous deviez |
| il doive | ils doivent |

There are a few irregular subjunctive forms:

1  The four verbs which do not end in 'ent' in the third person plural of the present.

| *avoir* | *être* |
|---|---|
| j'aie | je sois |
| nous ayons | nous soyons |
| ils aient | ils soient |

| *aller* | *faire* |
|---|---|
| j'aille | je fasse |
| nous allions | nous fassions |
| ils aillent | ils fassent |

2  The other verb which takes its imperative from the subjunctive (as do 'avoir' and 'être').

|  | *savoir* |
|---|---|
|  | je sache |
|  | nous sachions |
|  | ils sachent |

3  Two common auxiliary verbs.

| *pouvoir* | *vouloir* |
|---|---|
| je puisse | je veuille |
| nous puissions | nous voulions |
| ils puissent | ils veuillent |

4  Two impersonal verbs.

| *falloir* | *valoir* |
|---|---|
| il faille | il vaille |

*Perfect subjunctive*
This tense is formed in the same way as the perfect indicative, except that the present subjunctive forms of 'avoir' and 'être' are used.

| | *parler* | *aller* |
|---|---|---|
| e.g. | J'aie parlé | Je sois allé(e) |
| | tu aies parlé | tu sois allé(e) |
| | il ait parlé | il soit allé |
| | elle ait parlé | elle soit allée |
| | nous ayons parlé | nous soyons allé(e)s |

|                  |                        |
|------------------|------------------------|
| vous ayez parlé  | vous soyez allé(e)(s)  |
| ils aient parlé  | ils soient allés       |
| elles aient parlé | elles soient allées   |

*Imperfect subjunctive*
This tense is used infrequently (never in conversation) and then mainly
in the third person. Its stem is taken from the second person singular
of the past historic, to which 'se' is added to form the first person
singular.

|       |        |
|-------|--------|
| -se   | -sions |
| -ses  | -siez  |
| - ˆt  | -sent  |

e.g.                          *parler*

|                |                     |
|----------------|---------------------|
| je parlasse    | nous parlassions    |
| tu parlasses   | vous parlassiez     |
| il/elle parlât | ils/elles parlassent |

The third person singular is always the same as that of the past historic
with the addition of a circumflex accent and a 't' for 'er' verbs.

*Pluperfect subjunctive*
This tense is formed by using the imperfect subjunctive of the auxiliary
verb with the past participle.

e.g.    *finir*          *venir*
        il eût fini      il fut venu

## Use

The subjunctive in French could form the subject of a book in itself!
What follows are basic guidelines for the most common uses.

*Subjunctive as the main verb*
The only occasion when the subjunctive is used as the principal verb
in a sentence is when a command is given in the third person.

e.g.   Qu'il meure!          Let him die!

Notice that the subjunctive is still preceded by 'que'. There is an
exception to this in an expression beloved of French Presidents when
terminating a speech to the nation.

Vive la France!

*Subjunctive in noun clauses*
The subjunctive is required after certain verbs, providing that there is
a *change of subject* between the two verbs.
    These verbs can be grouped as follows:

1  Verbs expressing a wish or preference, or giving an order

   e.g. vouloir que    préférer que    ordonner que

       Example:        Je veux que tu **fasses** tes devoirs avant de sortir
                         I want you to do your homework before you
                         go out
                         *( Literally 'I wish that you do your homework')*

2  Verbs or phrases expressing an emotion

   e.g.

| | |
|---|---|
| regretter que | to be sorry that |
| être content/désolé que | to be pleased/very sorry that |
| être heureux/triste que | to be happy/sad that |
| avoir honte que | to be ashamed that |
| craindre que | |
| avoir peur que | to be afraid that/fear that |

       Example:        Je regrette qu tu n'**aies** pas reçu une bonne
                         note ce trimestre
                         I'm sorry you have not had a good mark
                         this term

Craindre and avoir peur require a further complication – the addition
of 'ne' before the subjunctive. The 'ne' is not translated.

       Example:        J'ai peur que tu ne perdes ton temps en
                         classe
                         I'm afraid you are wasting your time in
                         class

3  Verbs expressing some kind of doubt

   e.g.

| | |
|---|---|
| douter que | to doubt |
| il semble que | it seems that |
| il est possible que | it is possible that |

4  Certain verbs when used in the negative or interrogative

   e.g.

| | |
|---|---|
| penser que | to think that |
| croire que | to believe that |
| dire que | to say that |

       Example:        Je ne pense pas que tu **saches** l'importance
                         de tes examens
                         I don't think you know the importance of
                         your exams

5 Certain impersonal verbs

e.g.
| | |
|---|---|
| il faut que | it is necessary that |
| il est nécessaire que | it is necessary that |
| c'est dommage que | it is a pity that |
| il est temps que | it is time that |

Example: Il est temps que tu prennes tes études au sérieux

It's time you took your studies seriously

Remember that, if there is no change of subject between the verbs, there is no 'que', no subjunctive and the second verb is an infinitive.

Example: Oui Papa, mais mes devoirs sont faits et je veux **sortir**

Yes Dad, but my homework's done and I want to **go out**

*Subjunctive used in adverbial clauses*

Certain conjunctions must be followed by the subjunctive. Conjunctions always end in 'que'.

e.g.
| | | | |
|---|---|---|---|
| bien que } quoique } | although | pour que } afin que } | so that |
| avant que | before | pourvu que | provided that |
| jusqu'à ce que | until | sans que | without |

The following conjunctions require a 'ne' before the subjunctive:

de peur que } de crainte que } for fear that

à moins que      unless

Example: A moins que je **ne sois** à la maison à 11 heures, Papa sera furieux.

Unless I am home at 11 o'clock, Dad will be furious.

'Jusqu'à ce que' is reduced to 'que' after the verb 'attendre'.

'Bien que le film soit américain, il me plaît beaucoup.'

Example:         Attends que l'ouvreuse vienne pour lui de-
                 mander à quelle heure finit le film.
                 Wait until the usherette comes to ask her what
                 time the film finishes.

*Subjunctive used in adjectival clauses*
If a clause describes a noun which is qualified by a superlative, the
verb in the clause is in the subjunctive. Think of it as putting the noun
into a class of its own.

Example:         Le meilleur film que j'**aie** jamais vu était
                 français.

The best film I ever saw was French.

If the clause describes a noun which is indefinite or a negative, the verb in that clause is in the subjunctive.

Il y a un self où on **puisse** manger avant de rentrer?
Is there a self-service restaurant where we can eat before going home?

*Subjunctive used in concessive clauses*
The subjunctive is used in clauses beginning with 'whoever' (qui que) 'whatever' (quoi que) 'wherever' (où que) and similar constructions.

Example: Quoi que je **fasse**, Papa ne sera jamais content
Whatever I do, Dad will never be pleased

*Tense of the subjunctive*
The tense of the subjunctive is always dependent upon the tense of the main verb:

| main verb | subjunctive verb |
|---|---|
| Present | Present |
| Future | or |
| Perfect | Perfect |
| Imperfect | Imperfect |
| Conditional | or |
| Past Historic | Pluperfect |

## Exercise B

1 Rewrite the following sentences beginning with the words in brackets.

(a) L'Europe au XXI siècle peut devenir la première puissance mondiale.
  (Pensez-vous que .. .)
(b) La Communauté Européenne consistera de presque tous les pays du continent.
  (Les entrepreneurs sont contents que ...)
(c) Nous abandonnons une partie de notre pouvoir au profit d'un gouvernement européen.
  (Quelques politiciens britanniques ne veulent pas que ...)
(d) Le Marché Commun devient 'Forteresse Europe'.
  (Les Américains et les Japonnais ont peur que ...)
(e) Les entreprises savent exploiter les avantages d'un marché unique.
  (Il faut que ...)
(f) On est d'accord pour l'union économique; l'union politique reste toujours douteuse.
  (Bien que ...)

2    Change the following sentence by adding the words in brackets.

(a)    Le tunnel sous la Manche est le projet qui a capturé l'imagination
      de la nation.
          (le plus audace)

3    Vous avez l'opportunité de travailler et vivre en Europe. Croyez-
      vous qu'on doive se considérer européen plutôt que britannique?

# 20
# Helpful hints

## Mastering numbers

Understanding numbers is an important part of learning a language, and one of the first skills required when visiting a foreign country. Luckily the French number system is straightforward and easy to manipulate.

Numbers 1–16 are all different:

| | | | |
|---|---|---|---|
| 1 | un | 9 | neuf |
| 2 | deux | 10 | dix |
| 3 | trois | 11 | onze |
| 4 | quatre | 12 | douze |
| 5 | cinq | 13 | treize |
| 6 | six | 14 | quatorze |
| 7 | sept | 15 | quinze |
| 8 | huit | 16 | seize |

The only other numbers you need to learn are:

| | | | |
|---|---|---|---|
| 20 | vingt | 60 | soixante |
| 30 | trente | 100 | cent |
| 40 | quarante | 1000 | mille |
| 50 | cinquante | 1,000,000 | million |

The rest are combinations. Compound numbers up to 100 have their elements joined by a hyphen:

17 dix-sept        23 vingt-trois        99 quatre-vingt-dix-neuf

*except for*:

21, 31, 41, 51, 61, 71, where the two numbers are joined by 'et' and the hyphen disappears: 21 vingt et un, 71 soixante et onze

The arithmetic becomes more complicated after 69 (soixante-neuf):

| 70 | soixante-dix | 81 | quatre-vingt-un |
|----|--------------|----|------------------|
| 75 | soixante-quinze | 90 | quatre-vingt-dix |
| 80 | quatre-vingts | 95 | quatre-vingt-quinze |

Notice that quatre-vingts loses the final 's' whenever it is followed by another number. The same rule applies to the spelling of cent:

| 200 | deux cents | 201 | deux cent un |
|-----|------------|-----|--------------|

Don't forget: 0  zéro

Ordinal numbers (first, second, third, etc.) are formed by adding 'ième' to the cardinals (one, two, three, etc.): trois troisième (third).
There are a few spelling changes. The final 'e' of the cardinal is omitted:

quatre quatrième (fourth)

f changes to v:

neuf neuvième (ninth)

Note also:

| premier | (first) |
|---------|---------|
| second | (second) |
| vingt et unième | (twenty-first) |

Ordinals are also used for fractions (as in English):

$\frac{1}{5}$    un cinquième

Exceptions:

| $\frac{1}{2}$ | un demi (la moitié) |
| $\frac{1}{3}$ | un tiers |
| $\frac{1}{4}$ | un quart |

The decimal point in French is replaced by a comma (virgule):

2,45  =  2.45
deux virgule, quatre cinq  =  two point four five

### Exercise A

Read this story and then work out how the dervish solved the problem.

Un vieil Arabe, sur le point de mourir, fit venir ses trois fils pour leur dire comment ils devraient partager ses possessions après sa mort.

A l'aîné il dit 'Tu auras la moitié de tout ce que je possède'.
Au second fils 'Ta part sera un tiers'.
Et au cadet 'Pour toi un neuvième'.
Le vieux mourut. D'abord tout allait bien mais, quand on arriva aux chameaux, dont il y avait dix-sept, un problème se posa. Comment les partager sans couper en morceaux quelques-uns des animaux? L'aîné consulta un derviche bien connu dans la region pour sa sagesse.
'Faites ranger les animaux', ordonna celui-ci, et il ajouta son propre chameau aux autres.
'Maintenant que chacun prenne sa part', dit-il.
L'aîné en prit neuf (la moitié), le second fils six (un tiers) et le cadet deux (un neuvième). Le derviche reprit son propre chameau et s'en alla, laissant les trois frères intrigués mais contents.

*vocabulary*

| partager | to share |
|----------|----------|
| le cadet | the youngest |
| l'aîné | the eldest |
| le chameau | the camel |

**Encountering numbers**

Most times when you see a number it will be written as a figure and cause no problem. Spoken numbers, however, particularly if given rapidly, may be difficult to understand.

*Prices*
Listen for the word 'franc' which separates the francs from the centimes:

245F 70    deux cent quarante-cinq francs, soixante-dix

*Telephone numbers*
These are given in pairs:

25973806    vingt-cinq, quatre-vingt-dix-sept, trente-huit, zéro six

*Dates*
Listen for the word 'cent' which divides the date into two.

1789    dix-sept cent quatre-vingt-neuf *or* mil sept cent quatre-vingt-neuf

*Time*

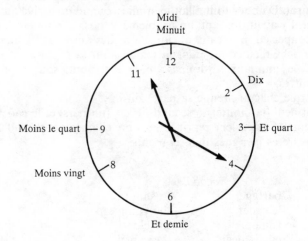

|                       |                              |
|-----------------------|------------------------------|
| Quelle heure est-il?  | Il est onze heures vingt.    |

Spelling points to remember:

|                    |                         |
|--------------------|-------------------------|
| 1 o'clock          | une heure               |
| 3.30               | trois heures et demie   |

*but*

|                    |                         |
|--------------------|-------------------------|
| 12.30 (noon)       | midi et demi            |
| 12.30 (midnight)   | minuit et demi          |

With digital watches and the twenty-four hour system, telling the time is more straightforward.

|        |                        |
|--------|------------------------|
| 17.30  | dix-sept heures trente |

## Exercise B

Rewrite this passage expressing the numbers in figures and translate it into English.

Entre dix-neuf cent quatre-vingt-cinq et dix-neuf cent quatre-vingt-sept, de cent dix mille à cent vingt mille d'emplois par an ont été perdus. Il y avait plus de deux millions de personnes au chômage. L'investissement industriel cette année a progressé de onze à douze pour cent, et les exportations manufacturières ont augmenté de sept pour cent en volume. On espère que c'est la fin du déclin de la désindustrialisation du pays.

## Getting the better of irregular verbs

No matter how much a pill is sweetened, at the end of the day there is always a bitter centre which has to be swallowed!

The smaller the core, however, the easier the pill is to swallow. When learning a new language, there is always some material which has to be learnt by heart. This is particularly the case with French irregular verbs but, providing you are aware of a few rules, the basic information you need to know in order to master them is small.

Learn the following principal parts of irregular verbs:

1  The present tense
2  First person singular of the future tense
3  First person singular of the past historic tense
4  The past participle

## 1  Present tense

This provides also:

| | |
|---|---|
| Imperative | tu, nous and vous forms without the subjects |
| Imperfect | stem the same as for 'nous'; endings 'ais', 'ais', 'ait', 'ions', 'iez', 'aient' |
| Present participle | stem the same as for 'nous'; exchange 'ant' for 'ons' |
| Present subjunctive | stem the same as for 'ils'; endings 'e', 'es', 'e', 'ions', 'iez', 'ent' |

(There are a few verbs whose imperatives, present participles and present subjunctive forms do not fit into this pattern, e.g. 'être', 'avoir', 'faire', 'aller'.)

## 2   First person singular of the future

The endings of the future tense do not vary from verb to verb. Once you know how the verb starts and remember the endings ('ai', 'as', 'a', 'ons', 'ez', 'ont') the tense is mastered.

Provides also:
Stem of the conditional tense. The endings change to those of the imperfect.

## 3   First person singular of the past historic

Again, once you know what set of endings the verb takes, there are no variations. The verb will belong to one of these groups:

| | | | | | |
|---|---|---|---|---|---|
| 'ai' | 'as' | 'a' | 'âmes' | 'âtes' | 'èrent' |
| 'is' | 'is' | 'it' | 'îmes' | 'îtes' | 'irent' |
| 'us' | 'us' | 'ut' | 'ûmes' | 'ûtes' | 'urent' |
| 'ins' | 'ins' | 'int' | 'înmes' | 'întes' | 'inrent' |

Provides also:
The imperfect subjunctive. Add 'se' to the 'tu' form. Endings 'sse', 'sses', ' ^ t', 'ssions', 'ssiez' 'ssent'.

## 4   Past participle

Provided you remember which auxiliary verb is required, any compound tense can be formed.

| | |
|---|---|
| Present of auxiliary + past participle | = Perfect |
| Imperfect of auxiliary + past participle | = Pluperfect |
| Future of auxiliary + past participle | = Future Perfect |
| Conditional of auxiliary + past participle | = Conditional Perfect |
| Past Historic of auxiliary + past participle | = Past Anterior |
| Present Subjunctive of auxiliary + past participle | = Perfect Subjunctive |
| Imperfect Subjunctive of auxiliary + past participle | = Pluperfect Subjunctive |

'Ça, je peux avaler!'

## Exercise C

Write out the principal parts of: écrire, prendre, voir, recevoir.

## Making the most of what you've got!

The written word is open to scrutiny. It can be studied at length to see whether it is right or wrong. Accuracy can be improved by checking carefully all written work.

Apply the following check-list to all written French and you will spot errors and know how to correct them.

*Check:*
1   All verbs to be sure that the tense is correct and the verb has the correct ending for the subject.
2   All adjectives and past participles for agreement. Don't forget the PDO rule.
3   All present participles. If one has been written after a preposition other than 'en', change it to an infinitive.
4   Any subjunctive. If you have used a subjunctive, what is the reason for it?
5   Any translation of 'you'. Should you use the familiar 'tu' form? If so have you kept to it in all its forms? Would 'on' be sometimes more appropriate?
6   The tense after 'quand', 'lorsque', 'dès que' and 'aussitôt que'. Should a form of the future or conditional be used?

**Exercise D**

Using the above check-list find the mistakes in the story and correct them.

Le fermier Deschamps avait besoin d'un nouveau tracteur. Il dit à son fils Jean, 'Demain vous allez en ville chercher une nouveau machine'.

Le lendemain Jean étais sur le point de partant quand sa mère appela de la cuisine 'Jean, apportes-moi un paquet d'aiguilles numéro cinq. Quand vous êtes en ville, vous verrez le magasin à côté de l'église. N'oubliez pas le numéro, cinq'.

En revenant à la ferme ce soir, Jean se dirigea tout de suite à sa mère.

'Mama, j'ai réussi à trouvant les aiguilles. Je les ai acheté dans le magasin près de l'église'.

Sa mère fut en train de féliciter Jean de sa bon mémoire quand le fermier entras.

'Eh bien, Jean,' dit-il', 'où est le tracteur?'

'Ah,' répondut Jean, tout confuse, 'je regrette Papa, je regrette infiniment, mais je l'aie tout à fait oubliée'.

# Part Four
Examinations and Useful Addresses

# 21
# Synopsis of major examinations

The attraction of having a certificate to show that you have reached a certain level of competence is a significant motivation factor for many students. The qualification can, of course, be very useful when seeking a job. Even those who come back to language learning in retirement may enjoy the challenge of taking an examination.

The range of examinations that you can take in French post GCSE is very wide. Besides the examination boards responsible for setting A and A/S Levels, there are other established commercial organizations which produce exams in French. Methods of testing vary and are continually being reassessed. If you wish to take an examination and have a choice, write away for a syllabus. The following information concerning the nature of the exams set by some of the bodies will help you to make up your mind.

## Associated Examining Board

### A Level

| | |
|---|---|
| Listening comprehension: | answers in English |
| Reading comprehension: | answers in English, translation into English, summary |
| Use of written language: | passage of English with questions in French, translation into French, summary, essay |
| Civilization, literature and culture: | two essays in French on two themes |
| Oral: | includes talk on topic set by Board |

### A/S Level in Contemporary French

| | |
|---|---|
| Listening comprehension: | as for A Level |
| Reading: | questions to be answered in English on six or seven short passages plus one long passage of French |

Oral:                              similar to A Level

**Certificate of Further Studies: French for Business**

This one-year course begins at GCSE, levels D or C, and aims at a standard less than halfway to A Level. Candidates are assessed on their ability to listen, speak, read and write in a business context. The oral component is assessed throughout the year by the class tutor.

**Cambridge**

---

**A Level**

| | |
|---|---|
| Speaking: | final oral examination or continuous assessment over a period with a shorter final test |
| Listening: | range of tests (gap filling, note-taking, questions, multiple choice) |
| Reading/writing: | two passages of French, one of English; range of tests (comprehension, comparison, summary, guided composition) |
| Essay: | subject set in March for examination in June |
| Coursework: | four items of work in French to be submitted |
| Thematic studies: | five themes set; three questions can be answered in French; one text from each theme may be taken into the exam |
| | the last two components may be taken separately or in a combined paper containing elements of both |

**A/S Level**

| | |
|---|---|
| Speaking | |
| | and two further papers chosen from: |
| Coursework | one or two pieces totalling approximately 1000 words |
| Listening | |
| Reading | |

## Joint Matriculation Board

### A Level

| | |
|---|---|
| Course work | internal assessment of three essays totalling approximately 2500 words |
| *or* | |
| Written paper | based on prescribed texts two questions to be answered in French, two in either English or French |
| Paper based on written material: | translation into English, translation into French, essay |
| Paper based on heard material: | answers mainly in English |
| Oral | |

### A/S Level

| | |
|---|---|
| Listening | |
| Reading or coursework: | two extended essays |
| Oral | |

## Oxford

### A Level

| | |
|---|---|
| Oral | |
| Reading: | answers in French, range of testing techniques |
| Listening: | candidates given individual tapes |
| Writing: | there are five options to taking this test – course work, a written examination, a viewing test (based on French video) or a combination of these; the paper is based on topics which are divided into literary and non-literary areas |

### A/S Level

| | |
|---|---|
| Oral | |
| Reading | |
| Listening: | individual tapes supplied |

## London

### A Level

*Syllabus A*

| | |
|---|---|
| Listening comprehension: | answers in English |
| Prescribed texts: | answers in English |
| *or* | |
| Prescribed topics: | answers in French |
| Guided writing and essay: | answers based on French stimulus material, prose and essay |
| Translation and reading Comprehension: | answers in English |
| Oral: | recorded, includes discussion of study extract prepared just before examination |

*Syllabus B*

| | |
|---|---|
| Listening comprehension: | common paper with syllabus A |
| Prescribed topics: | one French essay (500 words) |
| Guided composition: | French stimulus material on topics of current interest |
| Translation into French | |
| Translation from French | |
| Reading comprehension: | answers in English |
| Oral: | recorded, includes discussion of material prepared just before examination and a prescribed topic |

### A/S Level

| | |
|---|---|
| Listening comprehension: | answers in English |
| Reading comprehension: | answers in English |
| Writing: | in the form of a letter, report, leaflet or brochure |
| Oral: | discussion based on English stimulus material and a prepared topic – project based on a file of work |

Examinations set by the above Boards can lead to further study at a University or Polytechnic. Other examinations, often highly practical and vocational, are offered by the following boards.

## National Council of Vocational Qualifications

All examinations which are vocational rather than academic by nature will be scrutinized by the NCVQ, whose brief is to:

secure standards of occupational competence and ensure that vocational qualifications are based on them
approve bodies making accredited awards
design and implement a national framework for vocational qualifications
promote vocational education, training and qualifications.

National Vocational Qualifications will be available in approximately 80% of the courses open to post GCSE students and will be 'based on a clear specification of the competence and standards which industry and commerce say they require'. (*Oscar De Ville, NCVQ Chairman.*)

## Institute of Linguists

The Institute provides a range of public examinations in practical and vocational linguistic skills offered at five levels. All exams are based on tasks taken from the adult world.
*Preliminary* Three tests: reading, listening and oral.
*General* Roughly equivalent to GCSE (Grade C or above) or Scottish Standard Grade. Three tests: reading, listening, oral.
*Advanced* Roughly equivalent to 'A' level. Five tasks (modules), involving collating material from written and spoken sources and reporting on them, are set. Three must be passed within a period of 5 years. More than one module can be taken at a time.
*Intermediate* One test involving research, conducting an interview and writing up a report.
*Diploma* As with the Advanced level (IoL), 3 modules out of 5 have to be passed within 5 years. Language content equivalent to First Degree.

## London Chamber of Commerce and Industry Examinations Board

### Foreign Languages at Work (FLAW)

This is a teacher-assessed, course certification scheme which profiles a student's foreign language performance in up to 17 skill areas. The student accumulates a dossier of material (including tape recordings) on a variety of tasks (speaking, listening, using the telephone, reading a telex, filling in a form, etc.). S/he is assessed according to five levels of performance (level 5 being the highest). To qualify for a certificate, the student must reach level 2 or above in a minimum of ten activities. The emphasis is laid on speaking, listening and reading.

The organization also runs this other language exam

Foreign Language for Industry and Commerce (FLIC)

The LCCI, together with the Brussels Chamber of Commerce and German Chambers of Industry and Commerce, offers a combined set of modular awards for candidates seeking positions in Commerce/Industry in which they can offer bilingual commercial services.
There are three levels of certification:

Commercial Language Assistant Certificate
European Executive Assistant Certificate
Diploma in European Business Administration

## Royal Society of Arts (RSA)

RSA offers schemes which are vocationally orientated to assess, in a practical and realistic manner, competence to clearly defined criteria. The Board's certificate in Business Language Competence has five levels. All skills are tested within a business context with emphasis on oral competence. Later assessments allow students to specialize in a wide range of work areas such as tourism, banking, secretarial and export.

New developments in language learning testing are continually taking place and before deciding which examination is the most appropriate for you, write for the latest information.

# 22
# Useful addresses

## Examining boards

Associated Examining Board,
Stag Hill House, Guildford,
Surrey GU2 5XJ                                    Tel: 0483–506506

University of Cambridge,
Local Examinations Syndicate,
Syndicate Buildings,
1, Hills Road,
Cambridge CB1 2EU                                 Tel: 0223–61111

Joint Matriculation Board,
Manchester M15 6EU                                Tel: 061–9531180

University of London,
Schools Examinations Board, Stewart House,
32, Russell Square,
London WC1B 5DN                                   Tel: 071–636 8000

University of Oxford,
Delegacy of Local Examinations,
Ewert House,
Ewert Place,
Summertown,
Oxford OX2 7B2                                    Tel: 0865–54291

Welsh Joint Education Committee,
245, Western Avenue,
Cardiff CF5 2YX                                   Tel: 0222–561231

Scottish Examination Board,
Ironmill Road,
Dalkeith,
Midlothian
EH22 1LE                                          Tel: 031–6636601

Northern Ireland Schools Examinations Council,
Beechill House,
Beechill Road,
Belfast BT8 4RS                                    Tel: 0232–704666

Institute of Linguists,
24a, Highbury Grove,
London N5 2EA                                      Tel: 071–359 7445

London Chamber of Commerce and Industry,
Examinations Board,
Marlowe House,
Station Road,
Sidcup,
Kent DA15 7BJ                                      Tel: 081–302 0261

RSA,
Examinations Board,
Westwood Way,
Coventry CV4 8HS                                   Tel: 0203–470033

Business and Technician Education Council (BTEC),
Central House,
Upper Woburn Place,
London WE1H 0HH                                    Tel: 071–413 8400

City and Guilds of London Institute,
46 Britannia Street,
London WC1X 9RG                                    Tel: 071–278 2468

Oxford and Cambridge School Examinations Board,
Elsfield Way,
Oxford OX2 8EP                                     Tel: 0865–54547

Pitman Examinations Institute,
Catteshall Manor,
Godalming,
Surrey GU7 1UU                                     Tel: 0483–415311

Scottish Vocational Education Council (SCOTVEC),
Hanover House,
24 Douglas Street,
Glasgow G2 7NQ                                     Tel: 041–2487900

## Other useful addresses

The Central Bureau for Educational Visits and Exchanges,
Seymour Mews House,
Seymour Mews,
London W1H 9PE                                     Tel: 071–486 5101

A full list of all other commercial organizations which run examinations in French can be obtained from CILT.

The Centre for Information on Language Teaching and Research,
Regent's College,
Inner Circle,
Regent's Park,
London NW1 4NS                                  Tel: 071–486 8221

This office (5 minutes walk from Baker Street underground) houses an excellent library of books on all aspects of language learning.

Institut Français du Royaume Uni,
17, Queensbury Place,
London SW7 2DT                                  Tel: 071–589 6211

Ambassade de France,
(Service Culturel)
23, Cromwell Road,
South Kensington, London SW7 2EL                Tel: 071–581 5292

Centre National de Documentation Pédagogique,
29, Rue d'Ulm,
72530 Paris                              Tel: 010–331–46349000

BBC Enterprises Ltd,
Education and Training Sales,
Woodlands,
80, Wood Lane,
London W12 0TT                                  Tel: 081–576 2000

Thames Television International,
149, Tottenham Court Road,
London W1P 9LL                                  Tel: 071–387 9494

# Part Five
## Extra Practice

# Exercises

**Exercise 1**

Read the following passage:

La terre, est-elle vraiment en danger? Les pires cataclysmes, menacent-ils notre planète? Est-ce que les glaces polaires vont fondre et une bonne partie de nos territoires les plus riches sera inondée à cause du réchauffement du climat? Avec la disparition de la couche d'ozone, est-ce que les rayons ultra violets du soleil vont provoquer des cancers nouveaux? Suite à la destruction de la forêt amazonienne quel sera l'effet de l'accroissement rapide du taux du gaz carbonique contenu dans l'atmosphère?

Tous les hommes de science ne sont pas du même avis. Il y en a qui, avec beaucoup d'objectivité, s'efforcent de dissiper les fausses craintes. Mais il existe d'autres dangers, plus redoutables à long terme, comme l'érosion des sols. Tous les savants sont d'accord qu'il est urgent d'agir, mais pas n'importe comment.

(a) Make a list in English of the major imminent catastrophes which appear to be threatening the world.
(b) What possibly more dreadful danger is forecast?
(c) On what point are all scientists united?

Answer the following questions in French:
(d) Si le climat se réchauffe, qu'est-ce qui arrivera?
(e) Si les glaces polaires fondent, qu'est-ce qui arrivera?
(f) Si la couche d'ozone disparaissait qu'est-ce qui arriverait?
(g) Si la destruction de la forêt amazonienne continue, qu'est-ce qui arrivera?
(h) A votre avis, qu'est-ce qui cause l'érosion des sols?
(i) A votre avis, quel est le danger le plus redoutable?

| Ecole | Niveau | Points forts | Prix date d'inscription | Où s'inscrire |
|---|---|---|---|---|
| Science secours | Sixièmes à terminales. | 20 ans d'expérience dans l'encadrement scolaire. Cours hebdomadaires, stages de révision. | Toute l'année Stage Noël: 26 au 31 décembre 1.150 F à 1.200 F. | 68, rue du Commerce, Paris-15° **tél. 45.31.88.00,** et Paris-6°, Paris-16° |
| Cours Bac | Terminales A, B, C, D. | **Cours par petits groupes pour des périodes de 6 mercredis après-midi consécutifs entre novembre et avril.** | 750 F par période. | 4, rue Valette, 75005 Paris, **43.25.43.98.** |
| Cours boutard | Primaire aux terminales A,B,C,D. | **Enseignement à distance ou stages intensifs sur place.** | De 900 F à 1.200 F par matière. Inscription toute l'année. | 3, bd Morland, 75004 PARIS, **42.71.26.06.** |
| CDS | 6° à terminales. maths-physique, français-anglais, allemand-espagnol. | ● Ecoute de l'élève; ● suivi individuel; ● effectif réduit; ● cours dispensés par enseignants. | ● Base 100 F l'heure; ● stages: Toussaint, Noël, février, Pâques, été; ● soutien toute l'année. | 164, rue du Fbg-St-Honoré, 75008 PARIS Sur rendez-vous: **45.27.66.70.** |
| Collège A. Camus | Primaire, secondaire, supérieur. | **Rattrapage - soutien.** Méthodes - professeurs. Encadrement hebdomadaire. Stages vacances - Sport études. | Secrétariat ouvert du lundi au samedi. Prix moyen 1.200 F par stage. | 67, av. Mozart, 75016 PARIS **45.20.90.13.** |
| Cours Dom | Du CP à la terminale. Section spécialisée pour l'enseignement supérieur. | **Cours particuliers à domicile,** suivi hebdomadaire. Révisions intensives durant vacances sur **Paris et banlieue.** | De 95 F à 180 F/heure selon la classe. Inscriptions toute l'année. | 43, rue Planchat, 75020 PARIS, **43.70.99.66.** |
| P à D | Du C.P. à la terminale. | ● Sur un simple coup de fil, plus de 350 professeurs à votre disposition; ● enseignement personnalisé; ● stages intensifs. | De 80 F à 120 F de l'heure + frais de scolarité (300 F/trimestre). Documentation sur demande. | 3, rue Clément-Marot, 75008 PARIS, **47.23.53.52** |

## Exercise 2

Look at this list of intensive courses organized by private educational establishments and answer, in English, the questions below.

(a) (i)   What number would you telephone if you wanted to study on Wednesday afternoons?

   (ii)   During which months are the courses available?

   (iii)   How long does each course last?

(b) (i)   What age students would go to Science Secours for help?

   (ii)   How long has this establishment been operating?

(c) (i)   What subjects are offered at CDS?

   (ii)   When does it put on special courses?

(d) (i) Which establishment can call on the services of more than 350 teachers?

   (ii) What kind of tuition is available?

(e) (i) Which Baccalaureat courses are catered for at Cours Boutard?

   (ii) How much do they cost?

(f) (i) What are the particular merits of courses by the Collège A Camus?

   (ii) When could you phone the establishment?

(g) (i) What kind of tuition is available from Cours Dom?

   (ii) What do they organize in the holidays and where?

**Exercise 3**
(a) Role play:

You have just read the following advertisement in the newspaper and are phoning, from England, for further details. Your part of the conversation is outlined in English, between brackets.

---

**400K F + vehicule de fonction
+ avantages
Marketing
Communications
Manager
France.**

Notre client, une société multinationale américaine ayant une importante présence en Europe recherche un professionel de la communication marketing.

Vous devez maîtriser parfaitement l'anglais. Vous serez basé en France et représenterez une liaison importante entre les divisions françaises et européennes de la société. La société a une structure de gestion souple, ce qui signifie qu'une approche "hands on" est essentielle, une forte personnalité sera un atout majeur.

Vous devez posséder une grande expérience dans le domaine de la communication – PR, Expositions, Documentation, Publicité (une expérience avec une agence publicitaire sera un avantage). En tant qu'expert en communication, probablement le numéro 2 d'une organisation importante, vous serez naturellement en mesure de diriger et de faire la liaison entre le personnel du service de communication marketing à tous les niveaux, d'assurer une planification méticuleuse et de fournir un contrôle budgétaire du plus haut niveau.

---

Ce poste est d'une importance vitale, et la personne qui l'occupera devra avoir un sens affirmé de la responsabilité et posséder un dynamisme sans faille. Si vous possédez toutes les qualités et l'expérience nécessaires, téléphonez à André Bernard, au numéro (1) 45-02-14-39, ou bien envoyer votre candidature et les détails complets vous concernant, à: Novemploi, 7, Rue de Mont, 75830 Paris.

– *Allô oui, Novemploi.*
    (You want to speak to M. André Bernard)
– *C'est quel poste?*
    (You do not know the extension. You are ringing in response to an advertisement in an English newspaper)
– *Ben oui, je vous passe au service publicité. Ne quittez pas!*
– *Allô, service publicité. André Bernard à l'appareil.*
    (Introduce yourself and say that you are interested in the job of Marketing Communications Manager)
– *Où avez vous lu la publicité?*
    (In an English newspaper)
– *Vous êtes Anglais(e)?*
    (Yes, and you are telephoning from England)
– *Quelle expérience avez-vous dans le marketing?*
    (You have been sales manager for a small company for 4 years)
– *C'est tout?*
    (No, before that you had worked for 3 years as a journalist in advertising)
– *Intéressant. Quels sont vos diplômes, monsieur/madame?*
    (A Levels – like the Bac – in Maths, French and English and a diploma in Communications and Computer studies from Liverpool Polytechnic)
– *Pourquoi voulez-vous travailler en France?*
    (You like the French way of life and you have a French girlfriend/boyfriend)
– *D'accord. Vous avez des questions que vous voulez me poser?*
    (What does the company produce? When will the job start? Will there be much travelling outside France? Where would you be based?)
– *L'entreprise fabrique les tuyaux. Nous cherchons à remplir le poste aussitôt que possible. On voyage beaucoup en Europe, surtout en Allemagne, en Italie, au Royaume Uni et aux Etats Unis. Vous seriez basé(e) à Dijon.*
    (Thank him. You will send a CV shortly. Say goodbye and that you hope to make his acquaintance soon)
– *Au revoir, monsieur/madame. Merci d'avoir téléphoné.*

(b) Write your curriculum vitae for the job. There is a model for you to compare in the answer section. Include this information: you are 29, single and work in Coventry for Evans, a small engineering company which makes springs. You took a short course in marketing at Wolverhampton Polytechnic before joining Evans. You are fluent in French and can understand and speak German. You will be available in one month's time. You are interested in travel, languages and skiing.

**Exercise 4**

INSTITUTE OF LINGUISTS

EXAMINATIONS IN LANGUAGES FOR INTERNATIONAL COMMUNICATION

ADVANCED CERTIFICATE

MODULE C

TIME ALLOWED        TWO AND A HALF HOURS

INSTRUCTIONS FOR CANDIDATES

In this module you are required to produce a written communication in the foreign language in accordance with the instructions given in the task brief.

To help you to complete the module successfully, you should follow the sequence set out below.

1 Study the task brief carefully. This sets the scene for the task and explains exactly what you have to do.

2 Read the source materials in English and the foreign language and make notes to help you compile the communication.

3 Draft, write, revise and check your communication in the foreign language.

Ensure that the end product:

i)      passes on the required information clearly and unambiguously
ii)     is well organized and set out
iii)    is expressed in an appropriate style
iv)    generally conforms to the conventions for such communications in the foreign language

You may use dictionaries, as required.

## CANDIDATE'S TASK BRIEF

You work for a firm that manufactures drill parts for use in the metal industry. The firm is trying to break into the market in North and East Africa, and has therefore just appointed a French speaking Arab agent, M. Dahni, based in Marseilles.

You have just received a memorandum from your Manager, asking you to reply to M. Dahni's letter. Your task is to write this reply, incorporating the questions and comments contained in the memorandum.

You do not need to produce a letter heading in your handwritten version but you should ensure that you use appropriate opening and closing formulae. Your letter should generally conform to the conventions of French business correspondence, be well organized and usable as a real-life communication.

$2\frac{1}{2}$ hours are allowed for completion of the module.

## MATERIALS FILE

1   Memorandum from J. Holmes
2   Letter from M. Dahni
3   M. Dahni's list of African contacts

### MEMORANDUM

FROM:   J. Holmes

TO:                                                                     3rd May

------------------------------------------------------------

I have received this letter from our new agent in Africa, Dahni. He seems to think he can open up the markets for us there, but only if we drop our prices! Can you write back to him, thanking him for his letter, and to clarify the following:

– what is the top price he thinks we can ask and still remain competitive with the Italians?

– reassure him about our quality – the Germans definitely can't beat us

– he's not given us his exact dates in Algeria – we need to know for the telex

- whom exactly are we to contact in Tunisia – there's half a dozen on his list

- agree to send him some bits for the Moroccan market, but does he want them sending to him in Marseilles or can we send them directly to Morocco? If they go via Marseilles will that mean two lots of custom dues?

- he seems a bit worried about his contract. Tell him our solicitors are finalising it now and he should get it to sign by the beginning of next week.

| | |
|---|---|
| Mohammed Dahni | Ablett's Ltd |
| Ingénieur mécanicien | Unit 10 |
| Expert industries métallurgie | Barton Industrial Estate |
| 2 Rue de la République | Bradford Road |
| Marseille | Leeds LS19 5JG |
| | Marseille le 30 avril |

Cher Monsieur Holmes,

Je viens de recevoir votre courrier du 19 avril et je vous remercie pour la rapidité de votre réponse. Je vous remercie également pour la confiance que vous me faites en m'acceptant comme agent pour l'Afrique du Nord et l'Afrique de l'Est. J'espère que vous n'aurez pas à le regretter.

Pour l'Afrique du Nord, il y a un marché potentiel important, mais, vos prix sont supérieurs à ceux des Italiens qui sont à 1300.000 Lires. Cependant vos prix sont encore inférieurs à ceux de SCHNEIDER. Ici c'est plutôt une question de qualité. Je sais bien que votre qualité n'a rien à envier aux Italiens mais êtes-vous sûr d'en être au même niveau que les Allemands qui ont une très bonne réputation? En effet c'est seulement leur prix qui les empêchent d'emporter tout le marché, car, vue la situation économique des pays de Maghreb, on cherche toujours les prix les plus bas.

Actuellement il y a une demande de 60,000 mèches pour l'Algérie, mais je ne peux la faire passer que si vous pouvez réduire vos prix.

Je serai en Algérie avant la fin du mois de mai et je vais intervenir auprès de MARTIN de ENCIDEX pour qu'il s'intéresse davantage à vos mèches. Il faudrait donc que vous le contactiez par télex avant mon passage. De même, je serai à Tunis les 2, 3, et 4 juin où je verrais les 4 principaux tôliers. Il serait bon de les contacter avant mon passage.

Pour le Maroc, il faut d'abord attaquer les plus grosses tôleries. Ils vont d'abord tester la qualité, donc il vous faudra leur fournir un échantillon.

Je vous joins en annexe, la liste des tôleries à contacter en Afrique, et en priorité la Tunisie et l'Algérie.

Pour la bonne règle, je vous prie de bien vouloir me confirmer mon engagement comme agent de ABLETTS LTD, aux conditions dont nous sommes convenus.

Dans l'attente de vous lire,

Veuillez agréer, cher Monsieur Holmes, mes meilleurs salutations.

*M. Dahni*

M. DAHNI

## TOLERIES EN AFRIQUE

### *ALGERIE*

#### ALGER

Tôlerie Darbon
10 Rue de l'Est
(notre contact – M. Maignon)

Ets. Gromaire
8 Rue de France
(P. Gresset)

Tôlerie Encidex
20 Rue Arnaud Bisson
(D. Martin)

#### ORAN

Ets. Berchem
16bis Place J. Epinat
(M. Ng)

### *MAROC*

#### RABAT

Tôlerie Kien
85 Av. de la Libération
(M. Dohelec)

#### MEKNES

Tôlerie P. A. M.
12 Rue Persoz
(E. Messaoudah)

### *TUNISIE*

#### TUNIS

Tôlerie Gasen
23 Av. du Cimetière
(E. Alix)

Ets. Rongier
27 Bd. de Debes
(C. Carcat)

Tôlerie Lumirex
2 Rue Jean Jaurès
(M. Lichan)

Ets. Repam
83 Rue Flégier
(D. Guerin)

Ets. Guilloux
20 Rue du Bal
(G. Roy)

Ets. Jamnet
79 Rue Dufour
(S. Serel)

**Exercise 5**

## INSTITUTE OF LINGUISTS

## EXAMINATIONS IN LANGUAGES FOR INTERNATIONAL COMMUNICATION

## ADVANCED CERTIFICATE

## MODULE D

### TIME ALLOWED    2 1/2 HOURS

### INSTRUCTIONS FOR CANDIDATES

In this module you assume the role of someone who has been asked to research a particular topic using written sources in the foreign language and who then has to produce a written report in his/her first language.

To successfully complete the module, you should follow the sequence below:

1 Study your task brief carefully. This sets the scene for the task and explains what the report should contain.

2 Look through your dossier of written material and identify those parts of it which will be relevant to your report. Read these parts in detail and make notes.

3 Draft and write up your report.

No length is stipulated for the report but you should ensure that it is clearly laid out, readable and relevantly addresses the points indicated in the task brief. It should also be comprehensible to a person unfamiliar with the source material or the country to which the investigation relates.

You may consult dictionaries if you wish.

### CANDIDATE'S TASK BRIEF

You are working for a British publisher who is putting together a travel guide to Europe aimed specifically at the motorist. You are one of the team responsible for looking at France, and your particular brief is to investigate issues which are causing controversy. At the moment you are dealing with headlight colours and the Bison Futé operation. You have therefore obtained various documentation.

You are to produce a report which will form the basis of a chapter in the guide. Your report should include the following points:

i)    an explanation of 'Bison Futé' and the different ways in which it helps the motorist
ii)   the kind of operation mounted by 'Bison Futé' for holidaymakers returning home at the end of August
iii)  the relative merits of the motorways and the recommended alternative routes for returning holidaymakers
iv)   a brief survey of the headlamp colour controversy
v)    a clarification of the law for the British tourist

## DOSSIER

1   Extract from leaflet 'Bison Futé' (Ministère des Transports. Direction des routes)
2   'Dernière migration de l'été', *Auto Plus* 29.8.89
3   'La première vague de retours', *Auto Plus* 22.8.89
4   'Bison Futé' contre autoroute' *Auto Plus* 22.8.89
5   'A quand le phare blanc' (letter and reply from a magazine advice page)
6   'Phares blancs, phares jaunes', *Auto Plus* 29.8.89

*Item 1*

## BISON FUTÉ

**1   Les jours à éviter.**

Les jours rouges sont les jours de départ et de retour les plus chargés. Si vous pouvez vous abstenir de partir ces jours-là, vous préserverez vos nerfs et vous économiserez de l'essence.

Les jours oranges sont également très chargés mais toutefois moins difficiles.

| | **Jours de départ** | | **Jours de retour** | |
|---|---|---|---|---|
| orange | Samedi 5 juillet<br>Vendredi 11 juillet<br>Samedi 12 juillet | | Vendredi 1 août<br>Samedi 2 août<br>Jeudi 28 août | orange |
| rouge | Vendredi 1 août<br>Samedi 2 août<br>Dimanche 3 août | | Vendredi 29 août<br>Samedi 30 août | rouge |

Si malgré tout vous devez partir un de ces jours ...

---

**2** Partez à l'heure H.

---

Comme chaque année, Bison Futé a interrogé 100.000 personnes pour connaître les heures de départ et de retour des Français. L'analyse détaillée des informations ainsi recueillies permet de prévoir les meilleures heures de départ.

Elles vous seront données quelques jours avant les week-ends difficiles par la télévision, la radio et les journaux.

---

**3** Téléphonez à Bison Futé.

---

Avant de partir, ou même durant votre voyage, vous pourrez obtenir 24h sur 24 des informations sur l'état des routes, l'emplacement des bouchons, et les meilleurs itinéraires ... en téléphonant aux centres d'information routière.

Paris (1) 858.33.33　　　　Bordeaux (56) 96.33.33
Lille (20) 91.92.33　　　　 Lyon (7) 854.33.33
Marseille (91) 78.78.78　　 Metz (8) 762.11.22
Rennes (99) 50.73.93

---

**4** D'autres routes que les routes encombrées: les itinéraires bis.

---

Une carte vous indique en vert les itinéraires bis qui vous permettent d'éviter les encombrements des grands axes: lorsque vous verrez des panneaux, empruntez alors l'itinéraire bis indiqué par les flèches vertes.

> **5** **Autoroute du Soleil:**
> **une signalisation**
> **supplémentaire.**

Si vous rencontrez sur l'autoroute, ou sur la route qui y conduit un panneau jaune, c'est que l'autoroute est surchargée. Attention, dans ce cas surtout, votre intérêt est de prendre le prochain itinéraire bis fléché en vert.

> **6** **Du carburant**
> **sur les itinéraires bis.**

Les grandes marques d'essence Antar, Aral, B.P., Elf, Esso, Fina, Mobil, Shell, Total se sont associées à l'opération Bison Futé. C'est pourquoi certaines stations-service seront ouvertes la nuit pendant les périodes de forte circulation.

> **7** **Des points d'accueil**
> **pour s'informer.**

Sur les principaux axes routiers sont installés 75 points d'accueil. Vous y trouverez des informations concernant la circulation.

A votre demande, des hôtesses Bison Futé vous communiqueront gratuitement tous les renseignements utiles: possibilités d'hébergement, informations touristiques, adresses de garages, de médecins et de pharmacies de garde ... Vous pourrez également téléphoner. Les points d'accueil Bison Futé cont indiqués sur la carte par les signes

ⅰ **ⅰ** et sur la route par ce panneau.

N'hésitez pas à faire un pause détente,
vous serez toujours bien accueillis.

*Item 2*

# Dernière migration de l'été: attention danger

*Pour les spécialistes de la prévention routière, ces derniers jours d'août marquent l'ultime week-end à risques de l'été. Du 30 août au 3 septembre, six millions de vacanciers vont prendre la route du retour. Cinq jours d'intenses perturbations. Sachez choisir votre jour de départ.*

Derniers jours de soleil. Derniers départs. A partir de mercredi, la dernière transhumance des vacances d'été va s'amorcer. Les spécialistes du ministère des Transports se refusent pourtant à noircir le tableau puisque ces retours s'étaleront sur cinq jours. Cependant trois journées seront plus chargées que les autres.

Le drapeau orange flottera sur l'ensemble du territoire dès mercredi à partir de 15 h, mais il ne devrait pas y avoir en principe de difficultés majeures.

Pour ne pas rester prisonnier de la cohue, l'idéal est de partir avant le 30 août, ou après le 3 septembre, ou bien de rouler de nuit avec les risques que cela comporte.

# Les horaires à éviter

**Mercredi 30 août**

Toute la France de 15 h à 20 h

**Jeudi 31 aout**

Languedoc-Roussillon de 8 h à 14 h

Lyon de 10 h à 18 h

Bordeaux de 9 h à 15 h

Ile-de-France de 16 h à 21 h

**Vendredi 1er septembre**

Toute la France de 15 h à 20 h

**Samedi 2 septembre**

Toute la France de 8 h à 20 h

**Dimanche 3 septembre**

Toute la France de 12 h à 22 h

Jeudi 31, par contre, marquera un tournant important. C'est la fin du mois, et donc celle des locations. Les estivants de la "dernière minute" vont donc se rencontrer sur la route.

Accalmie vendredi, mais dès samedi l'orange risque fort de virer au rouge. Ce sera la journée choc des vacanciers qui auront pu prolonger leurs vacances jusqu'à la fin de la semaine, de la cohue des week-ends, mais aussi des vacanciers qui n'ont pris qu'une semaine de "court séjour".

### Traditionnels bouchons sur l'A 9 et l'A 10

L'essentiel des difficultés se situeront une fois encore sur l'autoroute A 9 entre Narbonne et Orange. Si vous voulez contourner ces difficultés, vous pouvez emprunter les itinéraires Bison Futé juste le temps de contourner le bouchon. N'empruntez surtout pas la nationale 113 qui longe l'autoroute A 9, elle connaît les mêmes encombrements.

Passé Orange sur l'autoroute A 7, la situation devrait être beaucoup plus favorable. Vous ne pourrez malgré tout pas échapper au traditionnel bouchon du tun-nel sous Fourvière. Si, lorsque vous êtes aux portes de Lyon, votre radio annonce 10 km de bouchon à l'entrée de Fourvière, comptez une heure pour voir le bout du tunnel.

Sur la côte aquitaine, les vacanciers connaîtront également leur lot d'embouteillages. Ceux qui remonteront de la côte basque risquent fort de rester bloqués sur la rocade de Bordeaux, puis sur l'autoroute A 10, dans les traditionnels bouchons des ponts d'Aquitaine et de la Dordogne.

Plus au nord, embouteillages en perspective dans la région de Tours, d'Orléans, ainsi qu'aux portes de l'Ile de France, au péage de Saint-Arnoult en Yvelines.

Les retours de Bretagne ne seront pas non plus épargnés par les difficultés, puisque les experts du ministère des Transports s'attendent à de très fortes perturbations sur les nationales 175, 176, et 24 dans la région de Plélan de Drand.

Des retours qui devraient, malgré tout, s'effectuer sans trop de problèmes, à moins que comme le redoutent les spécialistes du Centre National d'Informations Routières, des accidents ne viennent compliquer ces situations toujours très précaires. ∎

*Item 3*

# La première vague de retours des aoûtiens

## Les horaires à éviter

**Vendredi 25 août**

| Au départ de la côte méditerranéenne de 7 h à 18 h |
|---|

| Au départ de la côte aquitaine de 6 h à 15 h |
|---|

| Autour de Lyon de 11 h à 21 h |
|---|

**Samedi 26 août**

| Au départ de la côte méditerranéenne de 7 h à 18 h |
|---|

| Au départ de la côte aquitaine de 6 h à 15 h |
|---|

| Autour de Lyon de 11 h à 21 h |
|---|

**Dimanche 27 août**

| En Ile-de-France de 17 h à 21 h |
|---|

En orange, les heures pendant lesquelles le trafic sera dense. Légère accalmie en dehors de ces périodes. Par contre, la circulation sera dense aussi la nuit.

*Bison Futé a déterré sa hache de guerre pour la première vague des retours d'août. Objectif: éviter l'hécatombe de fin juillet. Deux jours à éviter impérativement: samedi 26 et dimanche 27.*

Pour quatre millions de vacanciers français, le prochain week-end marquera la fin des vacances.

Nostalgie certes, mais surtout de très sérieux problèmes de circulation en perspective, puisque les spécialistes du ministère des Transports prévoient deux journées orange dans le sens Sud-Nord, vendredi 25 et samedi 26.

Durant ces deux jours, évitez de prendre la route. On attend, en effet, autant de perturbations en 48 heures que lors du week-end du 15 août étalé sur 5 jours. C'est vendredi en milieu de matinée que débuteront les premiers problèmes.

Touchées en priorité, les zones proches de la Méditerranée et de l'Atlantique. Sur l'autoroute A 9, qui a battu cet été tous les records d'embouteillages entre l'échangeur d'Orange et la frontière espagnole, la situation sera épineuse dès 9 heures, et jusqu'à 15 heures.

Plus au nord, sur l'autoroute A 7, la remontée de la vallée du Rhône ne devrait pas poser de problèmes. Par contre, l'approche de Lyon sera, elle, très difficile. Les premiers bouchons avant le tunnel de Fourvière sont à craindre dès 11 heures, et pourront sévir tard dans la soirée jusqu'à 21 heures.

En revanche, les retours de la côte atlantique, via Bordeaux, seront plus fluides ... à condition toutefois d'éviter la tranche de 10 - 15 heures, notamment sur la rocade bordelaise A 630, et sur l'autoroute A 10 au niveau du pont d'Aquitaine.

Dans l'Ouest du pays, les retours de Bretagne seront ponctués d'embouteillages sur les nationales 175 et 176 dans les régions de Pontorson et Dinan.

Samedi 26, on prend les mêmes et on recommence! Ralentissements et embouteillages referont leur apparition sur l'ensemble du territoire aux mêmes heures que la veille.

## Double patience pour les Parisiens

Ces deux journées de folie devraient progressivement évoluer vers un retour au calme, sauf, bien sûr, en région parisienne. Dimanche soir, le trafic devrait, en effet, être très dense aux abords de la capitale avec des bouchons en perspective entre 18 et 21 heures. Par ailleurs, ce sont des travaux qui entraîneront des ralentissements. Ainsi l'autoroute de Normandie sera pénalisée par des travaux nocturnes. La circulation y sera réduite à une voie toutes les nuits dans le sens province - Paris, entre Rocquencourt et Vaucresson. L'autoroute A 6 vers Fresnes, risque, elle aussi, d'être encombrée, puisque la circulation s'y fera sur trois voies à largeur réduite.

Prudence donc pour ce week-end de retours, spécialement la nuit où le trafic ne désarmera pas. ∎

*Item 4*

# Bison Futé contre autoroute : le match retour

*"Bison Futé" ou l'autoroute? Nous avions fait un premier test le 30 juin dernier entre Paris et Nice. L'autoroute avait gagné: l'équipage qui l'avait empruntée était arrivé 7 heures plus tôt que la voiture pratiquant l'itinéraire bis. Le 30 juillet nous avons donné à notre "Peau Rouge" national une nouvelle chance. Deuxième déconvenue! De nos deux équipages, celui qui a suivi les pistes de "l'indien" est resté sur la route 4h45 de plus que l'autre...*

**Même bouchée sur 106 km, l'autoroute fait gagner du temps**

AUTO PLUS No 50 - 22.08.89 -

# Notre tableau de marche

## Par l'autoroute

### Douze millions de vacanciers sur le retour

Ni les conseils d'étalement des départs de Bison Futé, ni les images spectaculaires à la télévision de bouchons ou de collision n'y ont changé quelque chose. A l'heure où nous quittons Nice, c'est déjà la cohue. Pour éviter les bouchons au péage de l'autoroute, des employés distribuent eux-même les tickets.

**9 h à 11 h**

## Par Bison Futé

### Attention prudence!

Nous voilà en route pour la deuxième partie de notre grande aventure estivale. Nous quittons Nice sous le soleil, direction l'autoroute. La circulation est assez dense, et il convient d'être prudent. Difficile de garder une vitesse stable, la vigilance est donc de rigueur. A 11 heures pile nous arrivons au péage d'Aix où il n'y a pas d'attente.

## Ralentissements inexpliqués

Le trafic est très dense et nous roulons en "accordéon": tantôt à 30 km/h, tantôt à vitesse normale. La raison? Souvent inconnue. De temps en temps, c'est une bretelle qui déverse son flôt de voitures, ou un rétrécissement de 3 en 2 voies. Mais bien souvent, il n'y a ni accident, ni bretelle, ni entonnoir ...

## Ambiance vacances sur les aires de repos

Le trafic est toujours très dense, et pourtant cela roule. Sur les aires de repos, tout le monde pique-nique, ou se douche! Il fait quarante degrés à l'ombre, et rester dans sa voiture tient de l'exploit. Au détour des parkings, des enfants en maillot de bain continuent de jouer au ballon ou au badmington. Ce n'est plus les vacances, et pourtant chacun essaie de l'oublier.

## Lyon et ses bouchons

A l'approche de Lyon, le trafic commence déjà à se ralentir. A la radio, on annonce 100 km de bouchons. Cette fois nous n'y échapperons pas. Des itinéraires de délestage obligatoire ont été mis en place par la police. Nous devons traverser Lyon! Dans la ville, les accrochages se succèdent. Le bouchon semble indévissable. Pourtant, d'après la radio, Fourvières est maintenant dégagé.

## 11 h à 13 h   Bison Futé, nous revoilà!

Tout avait trop bien commencé. A une quarantaine de kilomètres de Salon de Provence, nous nous retrouvons dans un bouchon. Heureusement cela ne dure pas trop longtemps. A cet endroit, nos trois voies se transforment en deux voies, ce qui a donné lieu à un léger accrochage entre trois voitures. C'est à 11 h 40 que nous atteignons la sortie de Cavaillon où notre itinéraire bis commence.

## 13 h à 15 h   Bison Futé et les Belges ...

Après avoir fait deux fois le tour de Valréas, nous décidons de faire une pause-déjeuner à la Bégude de Mazenc. C'est là que nous rencontrons Etienne et Mariette, un couple de Belges, qui eux aussi suivent Bison Futé. En Belgique, une grande publicité est faite pour cet itinéraire. Visiblement, ils en sont satisfaits ... bien qu'ils se soient déjà perdus plusieurs fois!

## 15 h à 17 h   Une allure d'escargot

Nous ne rencontrons pas beaucoup de monde, mais sur ces routes tortueuses, il suffit d'une caravane pour que l'allure devienne quasiment nulle. Doubler, il n'en est pas question, la chaussée est trop étroite. Quand ce ne sont pas les caravanes, quelques voiturettes en vadrouille en ce samedi après-midi se chargent de nous ralentir.

## Où il faut prendre son mal en patience

Nous en sommes enfin sortis! Bilan: 60 km parcourus en 2 heures. Etrangement, c'est sur la voie de droite que l'on circulait le plus vite. En matière de circulation, aucune logique n'est applicable! Après ces deux longues heures de bouchon, hommes et machines sont fatigués. Les aires de repos, comme celles de Beaune, sont encombrées, et les pompes à essence inaccessibles.

## Les fous du volant

Nous ne les avions pas encore rencontrés, mais là nous sommes servis. Quelques "chauffeurs d'élite" se sentent pousser des ailes à l'approche de la capitale. Quel que soit leur chargement, de joyeux pères de famille lancent leur voiture d'une voie à l'autre. Tout est bon pour doubler: à droite, sans clignotant, par la bande d'arrêt d'urgence. Bilan: 102 morts.

## Paris, nous voilà!

Paris approche et le trafic s'intensifie de nouveau. Pourtant les portes de Paris sont fluides. C'est donc un jeu d'enfant d'aller de la porte d'Orléans à la place de l'Opéra où s'achève notre voyage. A 22 heures, la boucle est bouclée. Nous avons couvert 949 km en 13 heures, soit une heure de plus qu'à l'aller. Bison Futé, quant à lui, n'est pas encore arrivé ...

## 17 h à 19 h   Perdues dans Lyon

Problème à l'approche de Lyon: il n'y a plus aucune flèche verte. De plus, nous tombons pile devant l'entrée du stade Edouard Herriot, où se déroule le match Lyon-Toulouse! De déviation en déviation, nous perdons pratiquement 1 heure. 30 km plus loin, nous retrouvons ENFIN un panneau d'"itinéraire bis", par le plus grand des hasards ... et grâce à notre boussole!

## 19 h à 21 h   Etape gastronomique

Décidément la chance n'est pas avec nous. A Pont de Vaux, nous tombons sur une nouvelle déviation. La route est barrée pour cause de travaux, il faut se débrouiller pour récupérer Bison Futé. Après toutes ces contrariétés, nous prenons la décision de nous arrêter pour diner dans une charmante auberge à Tournus. Nous ne voulons pas risquer de trouver porte close plus loin.

## 21 h à 23 h   Trois voies dans la nuit

La nuit est tombée lorsque nous reprenons la route. Nous empruntons la N 80 en direction du Creusot et enjambons un bref instant l'autoroute. La circulation y est très fluide ... Heureusement pour nous, la route nationale que nous suivons est assez agréable. Pourvue de trois voies, la circulation y est dense, mais nous pouvons enfin rouler à une allure convenable.

## Paris plus désert qu'un retour de week-end

Hors de question d'aller nous coucher tout de suite. Nos petits camarades sont encore sur la route. Nous prenons donc patience en buvant un café. Dans Paris vidé de ses habitants, les touristes sont rois. Appareil photo autour du cou, ils déambulent au milieu des rues, profitant de l'absence de circulation. Il n'auront pas la possibilité de recommencer très souvent!

## Bison Futé pointe le bout de son nez

"L'indien" de ministère des Transports s'est encore "planté". L'autre équipage pointe le bout de son nez 4 h 45 après notre arrivée. Exténuées, fourbues, nos deux reporters ont des samsonites sous les yeux. Certes, elles n'ont pas rencontré le moindre bouchon, mais cela valait-il les 17 h 45 passées à se battre avec les lacets des petites routes de campagne?

**23 h à 1 h**

## La route de cauchemar

A Autun, nouveau problème de fléchage. Notre objectif est Saulieu, mais rien ne nous indique la bonne direction. Nous nous retrouvons tout de même sur la D 4 déserte, sans marquage au sol, à moitié défoncée ... Déjà, il y a un mois, lors de notre trajet "aller" elle était dans le même état! Enfin à 0 heure, nous entrons sur l'autoroute à Avallon. Notre calvaire est fini.

**1 h à 03 h**

## Record battu!

Dans le sens province-Paris, l'autoroute est dégagée. Dans l'autre sens, par contre, le flot des vacanciers qui vont rejoindre leur lieu de villégiature est assez impressionnant. L'entrée dans Paris se fait sans problème, et à 2 h 45 nous arrivons place de l'Opéra. Belle performance: nous avons couvert la distance en 17 h 45, contre 19 heures à l'aller!

Il est 02 h 45 du matin place de l'Opéra à Paris quand apparait l'équipage Bison Futé. Pour nos deux reporters, c'est presque un exploit, elles ont mis 01 h 15 de moins qu'à l'aller!

| **Autoroute** | **Bison Futé** |
|---|---|
| *avantages* | |
| Rapidité | Itinéraire touristique |
| Confort | Coût peu élevé |
| Sécurité | |
| *désavantages* | |
| Bouchons | Routes dangereuses |
| Prix prohibitifs | Peu d'infrastructures d'accueil |
| | Longueur du trajet |
| | Isolement la nuit |

**Budget Autoroute**

- Kilomètres parcourus: 949 km
- Consommation totale: 88 litres à 5,57 F le litre (moyenne sur ce parcours), soit 490,16 francs.
- Consommation moyenne: 9,271/100 km
- Péage: 254 francs
- Total: 744,16 francs

**Budget Bison Futé**

- Kilomètres parcourus: 1 043 km
- Consommation totale: 89 litres à 5,20 F le litre (moyenne sur ce parcours), soit 462,80 francs.
- Consommation moyenne: 8,531/100 km
- Péage: 109 francs
- Total: 571,80 francs

*Item 5*

# A quand le phare blanc?

M on fils s'est fait arrêter pour avoir circulé en moto avec un phare blanc. On lui a infligé une amende de 450 F. J'avais pourtant lu dans une revue qu'il était récemment paru un décret qui les autorisait. Qu'en est-il?

Mme Vernay
95190 Goussainville

A notre connaissance aucun décret n'a encore été instauré qui autorise les phares blancs sur les véhicules immatriculés et circulant en France. Seul les voitures étrangères en transit, ou les véhicules français circulant à l'étranger ont, pour l'instant, le droit d'utiliser ces phares. A l'horizon de 1993, le choix devrait être laissé à tous les usagers au sein de la communauté européenne. Mais pour l'instant, l'utilisation de phares blancs est encore interdite aux Français circulant en France.

*Item 6*

# **V**otre sécurité

## La politique de l'autruche

### Par François Granet

# Phares blancs, phares jaunes :
# le brouillard s'épaissit

*A l'aube de 1993, un sujet déchaîne toutes les passions. Nos voitures vont-elles éclairer la nouvelle Europe en blanc ou en jaune? La réponse reste dans le brouillard. Le blanc éclaire mieux, mais le jaune fatigue moins les yeux. De toute façon, nos gouvernants ne sont pas pressés de changer la réglementation.*

**S**i en 1993, l'Europe doit devenir, en théorie, une et indivisible, côté éclairage, l'harmonisation n'est pas de mise. L'application d'une directive européenne du 27 juillet 1976 mettrait pourtant tout le monde d'accord. Ce texte stipule que: "Les couleurs de la lumière émises par les feux de route et les feux de croisement des voitures peuvent être le blanc ou le jaune" ... Malheureusement, ce texte n'est pas une loi. Il ne s'applique que si les Etats n'ont pas déjà pris des dispositions contraires. C'est en Europe le cas pour deux pays: la France et la R.F.A. Partout ailleurs, phares blancs et jaunes sont autorisés.

## Un éclairage jaune pour des raisons militaires!

Alors que toutes les voitures étaient équipées de phares blancs, la France rend obligatoire en 1939 l'éclairage jaune sur les véhicules (articles R.83 et R.84 du code de la route). Et cela pour des raisons militaires. Il semble en effet que ce soit l'Etat Major qui ait demandé au gouvernement que les véhicules français soient équipés de phares jaunes, afin de pouvoir les différencier des véhicules allemands en cas de conflit. L'ambiance n'était pas alors à la franche camaraderie entre nos deux pays! Il fut donc interdit d'éclairer blanc en France ... tandis que les Allemands bannissaient les phares jaunes.

Les années ont passé, nous sommes réconciliés depuis longtemps avec nos voisins d'outre-Rhin, mais la loi est restée. Les Français refusent toujours les phares blancs, et les Allemands abhorrent le jaune. Le respect de la directive européenne du 27 juillet 1976 par la France et la R.F.A. n'est donc pas pour demain.

Le problème de l'éclairage blanc ou jaune est devenu un véritable sujet tabou dans les hautes sphères du pouvoir. Comme si les gouvernements français et allemands ne voulaient pas perdre la face en se pliant à la directive européenne. Il est de toute façon certain qu'aucun changement de réglementation n'interviendra avant l'ouverture du grand marché européen le 1er janvier 1993. Il n'existe en effet actuellement aucune négociation inter-gouvernementale au niveau communautaire pour résoudre ce problème.

Quant aux autres pays européens, si leurs véhicules sont tous équipés de phares blancs, c'est tout simplement parce qu'une ampoule blanche est plus facile à fabriquer qu'une jaune. Les équipementiers et les constructeurs automobiles réalisent donc tous des économies!

### Ne pas confondre vue et éblouissement

La lumière blanche éclaire-t-elle mieux que la lumière jaune? Pas forcément! Une voiture équipée de phares jaunes éclaire avec moins d'intensité pour une raison très simple: une ampoule jaune est en fait une ampoule blanche sur laquelle on a fixé un globe jaune. Or cette pellicule jaune agit comme un filtre, et "bouffe" de la lumière (jusqu'à 33% de perte de puissance). Un phare jaune envoie donc moins de radiations lumineuses qu'une ampoule blanche, dépourvue, elle, de filtre.

---

### Et vous, qu'en pensez-vous?

Le blanc vous éblouit? Le jaune éclaire mal?
Dans trois ans, à l'ouverture des frontières européennes, voulez-vous que les voitures européennes éclairent blanc ou jaune? Ecrivez-nous pour nous donner votre avis.

**Exercise 6 (RSA, Level 2): Part 1 – Reading Skills**

You are planning to spend a fortnight's holiday on the island of Corsica in the Mediterranean Sea. You write off to the French National Tourist Board to get information on the island and on tourist accommodation there.

Extracts from the leaflets that you receive from the Tourist Board form the Candidate Reading Material.

A. First look at the introduction to Corsica (Item A of the Candidate Reading Material) and then answer in English the questions below in the spaces provided.

1  Give details of four natural features of the coastal areas of Corsica.

   (*a*) ................................................................................................................

   (*b*) ................................................................................................................

   (*c*) ................................................................................................................

   (*d*) ................................................................................................................

2  Name two types of wildlife to be found on the island.

   (*a*) ................................................................................................................

   (*b*) ................................................................................................................

3  Give below details of two natural features of the upper mountain areas of Corsica besides the one already given in the table below.

| (*a*) FORESTS. |
| --- |
| (*b*) ........................................................................................ |
| (*c*) ........................................................................................ |

B. Now look at the information on types of tourist accommodation available in Corsica (Item B of the Candidate Reading Material). Answer in English the questions below in the spaces provided.

4  What is said about hotel accommodation (a) in season (b) out of season?

   (*a*) ................................................................................................................

   (*b*) ................................................................................................................

5  What exactly are "Gîtes Ruraux"?

   ................................................................................................................

   ................................................................................................................

**6** Which *two* of the following statements are true about "Chambres d'Hôte"? (tick *two* of the boxes below: leave others blank)

|  | tick below (√) |
|---|---|
| ACCOMMODATION IS BED AND BREAKFAST ONLY |  |
| HALF-BOARD OR FULL-BOARD IS AVAILABLE |  |
| ACCOMMODATION IS FOR FAMILIES OF FARM WORKERS ONLY |  |
| THIS TYPE OF ACCOMMODATION IS NOT YET WIDELY AVAILABLE IN CORSICA |  |
| THIS TYPE OF ACCOMMODATION IS AVAILABLE BOTH IN TOWNS AND IN THE COUNTRYSIDE |  |

**7** What is said about people who go camping, or who wish to go camping, in Corsica without using official or purpose-built camp-sites? Give *two* details.

(*a*) ................................................................................................................

(*b*) ................................................................................................................

**8** What arrangements for meals are available in the "Villages de Vacances"? Give *two* details.

(*a*) ................................................................................................................

(*b*) ................................................................................................................

**C.** Enclosed with the information that you receive is a leaflet issued by the "Ministère de l'Intérieur et de la Décentralisation". The contents of this leaflet appear in Item C of the Candidate Reading Material. Look at this and answer in English the questions below in the spaces provided.

**9** What *two* pieces of advice are given specifically about motorway driving?

(*a*) ................................................................................................................

(*b*) ................................................................................................................

**10** Give details of *one* piece of advice given for each of the groups below.

(*a*) Bathers in general (on any type of beach) ......................................

................................................................................................................

(*b*) Children on the beach ...........................................................................

................................................................................................................

(*c*) Windsurfers ...................................................................................................

..................................................................................................................................

**11** What *two* objects should you take with you when going off into the mountains?

(*a*) ...........................................................................................................................

(*b*) ...........................................................................................................................

**12** What are you and your friends advised to do before going off into the mountains? (Give *two* details)

(*a*) ...........................................................................................................................

(*b*) ...........................................................................................................................

**13** You are told to take strict fire precautions when in forests. Name at least *one* thing that you are told NOT to do when visiting such places.

..................................................................................................................................

*Item A*

# Informations pratiques

## LA CORSE C'EST:

*1,000 km de sable, de criques, et de golfes.*
*Aux longues bandes de sable de la Côte Orientale*
*s'opposent les petites criques mi-rocheuses,*
*mi-sableuses des golfes de la Côte Occidentale,*
*les plages plus sauvages du Cap Corse,*
*ou les falaises calcaires de l'extrême Sud.*

*La nature partout reine est encore respectée, paysages magnifiques, fleurs étranges avec une exceptionnelle flore indigène, mais aussi des bêtes qui y vivent: aigles, truites, et sangliers.*

*Entre 500 et 800 m règne le maquis aux plantes aromatiques embaumant l'air. Au-dessus de 800 m, apparaissent les ruisseaux à truites, les forêts, les lacs nichés parmi les rochers, les sommets enneigés de novembre à mai.*

*La corse c'est aussi une vieille terre chargée d'histoire aux nombreux vestiges, depuis la Préhistoire, l'Antiquité Grecque en passant par les nombreux souvenirs de l'Empereur Napoléon 1$^{er}$, né à Ajaccio.*

*Item B*

# VOTRE HÉBERGEMENT EN CORSE

## Hôtels

Le parc régional en hôtels est, dans sa très grande majorité, récent et de bonne qualité.

La Corse offre au total près de 28,000 lits d'hôtels concentrés, pour l'essentiel, sur le littoral, mais un effort est réalisé en faveur de la petite hôtellerie de l'intérieur. D'ores et déjà, plusieurs établissements de qualité sont prêts à accueillir les amoureux de "l'autre Corse".

En saison, il est recommandé de réserver à l'avance ses chambres. Par ailleurs, une réduction sensible est consentie hors saison par la plupart des hôteliers.

### Locations de vacances en espace rural

Les structures d'accueil du "Tourisme Vert" sont présentes dans l'île même si la capacité offerte n'est pas encore à la mesure des possibilités de la montagne corse.

### GITES RURAUX

Le gîte rural est une maison meublée et équipée située près d'une ferme ou d'un village. Aménagé en fonction de la "Charte des Gîtes de France", il est classé en fonction du degré de confort et de la qualité de l'environnement (1, 2 ou 3 épis). Il est loué à la semaine.
Les gîtes ruraux de Corse représentent une capacité d'accueil d'environ 1,187 lits.

### CHAMBRES D'HOTE

Ce sont des chambres aménagées chez des agriculteurs pour accueillir promeneurs et touristes et leur offrir le coucher et le petit déjeuner. Cette forme d'hébergement en milieu rural est encore peu répandue en Corse.

Un guide de l'accueil rural en Corse est édité annuellement par le Comité Régional des Gîtes Ruraux et l'Agence Régionale du Tourisme et des Loisirs, 22, cours Grandval, B.P. 19 - 20176 AJACCIO CEDEX.

## Camping

La Corse est accueillante pour les campeurs qui y trouvent un choix très varié de terrains aménagés, que ce soit en montagne, en forêt ou au bord de la mer.
Près de 30,000 campeurs peuvent être accueillis dans les 116 terrains existants et il se crée chaque année de nouveaux équipements (terrains, aires naturelles de camping).
L'amoureux de la nature ne doit pas ignorer que le camping sauvage — tentation permanente en Corse — constitue un réel danger pour les sites.
Aussi le camping est-il interdit sur les rivages de la mer. Dans tous les cas, hors de campings aménagés, l'autorisation du propriétaire du terrain est nécessaire.
Un guide des terrains de camping-caravaning autorisés est édité annuellement par l'Agence Régionale du Tourisme et des Loisirs, 22, cours Grandval, B.P. 19 - 20176 AJACCIO CEDEX.

**Fédération Régionale de l'Hôtellerie de Plein Air de la Corse-du-Sud, Camping "U Prunelli" - 20166 PORTICCIO.**

**Fédération Régionale de l'Hôtellerie de Plein Air de la Haute-Corse, Camping "Monte Ortu" - 20260 LUMIO - Tél.: 95.60.73.93.**

### Villages de vacances

Une cinquantaine de villages de vacances offrent des séjours variés à un prix forfaitaire comportant la fourniture de repas ou des moyens individuels pour les préparer et l'usage d'équipements collectifs permettant des activités de loisirs sportifs et culturels. Certains sont réservés aux naturistes.

Un guide des villages de vacances et du naturisme est édité annuellement par l'Agence Régionale du Tourisme et des Loisirs de Corse, 22, cours Grandval, B.P. 19 - 20176 AJACCIO CEDEX.

*Item C*

## Sur la route

Votre véhicule est-il en bon état?
(freins, pneumatiques).
Vous conduisez? Alors soyez
*sobre, attentif, prudent.*
Respectez le code de la route.

Sur les autoroutes, respectez les distances et, sauf nécessité, n'empruntez pas la bande d'arrêt d'urgence.
*L'important c'est d'arriver.*

## Au bord de l'eau

Sur les plages surveillées, observez les consignes données. Baignades non surveillées: un danger est toujours possible. Ne vous baignez jamais seul. Ne quittez pas vos enfants des yeux, mêmes s'ils savent nager.

Plongeurs, méfiez-vous des obstacles non apparents. Véliplanchistes, équipez-vous d'un harnais, d'un gilet de sauvetage et d'une combinaison isothermique.

## A la montagne

Une randonnée, une escalade se préparent. Tenez compte des bulletins météo.

Votre équipement doit être parfaitement adapté. Prévoyez toujours une fusée de détresse et une lampe électrique. Souvenez-vous du signal de détresse (les 2 bras levés formant un Y avec le corps).

*Ne partez jamais seul ...* et soyez accompagné de personnes expérimentées. Recourez aux guides et aux accompagnateurs.

*Prévenez toujours quelqu'un* de votre itinéraire, de la composition de votre groupe et de l'heure de votre retour.

## En forêt

La forêt nous donne son bois, ses fleurs, ses champignons, ses ombrages et l'air pur. Elle protège le sol contre l'érosion. Elle est l'habitat ou le refuge d'une grande diversité d'animaux. Elle est pour l'homme un espace de silence, de détente et d'activités sportives.

Mais *la forêt est fragile et vulnérable. Respectez-la.*

Ne détruisez pas les végétaux. N'abandonnez pas de déchets.

*ENFIN*
*SOUVENEZ-VOUS*
*QUE LE FEU*
*EST L'ENNEMI*
*DE LA FORÊT!*

Évitez de fumer.
N'allumez pas de feu.

Et si vous êtes témoin d'un *feu naissant,* donnez *immédiatement l'alarme: mairie, sapeurs-pompiers* (tél. 18 ou numéro local), *gendarmerie ...* et commencez la lutte en frappant la frange du feu avec une pelle, un branchage, en y jetant de la terre ou mieux de l'eau.

*Chaque année,* outre les pertes en vies humaines qu'il provoque et les risques particuliers qu'il fait encourir aux sapeurs-pompiers, le feu détruit des dizaines de milliers d'hectares.

*Cela coûte très cher à l'État, aux régions, aux départements, aux communes ...*
*... et en définitive à chacun d'entre nous.*

*suivez ces conseils pour revenir sain et sauf*

### BONNES VACANCES

* Pour toute information complémentaire, adressez-vous à la Direction Départementale de la Protection Civile à la Préfecture du département de votre résidence.

Numéro(s) de téléphone des moyens de secours locaux:

|  |  |  |
|---|---|---|
|  |  |  |

*(A compléter vous-même).*

**Exercise 6 (RSA, Level 2): Part 2 – Listening Skills (with writing option)**

A.  You are on holiday in Corsica staying in a small villa in a holiday village complex in the south of the island. On the morning following your arrival there is a small informal welcome drink for those who have just arrived. A young lady from the reception bureau at the holiday complex is there and starts a short introductory talk.

Listen to what she says and then answer in English, in the spaces provided, the questions that follow.

1   Give details of what the numbers below refer to:

170 = ..............................................................................................................

 83 = ..............................................................................................................

180 = ..............................................................................................................

 80 = ..............................................................................................................

2   Give *two* pieces of information mentioned about the sea that would be of interest to swimmers.

(*a*) ............................................................................................................

(*b*) ............................................................................................................

3   Name *two* types of sport mentioned.

(*a*) ............................................................................................................

(*b*) ............................................................................................................

4   Give *two* details of the mountain areas of Corsica.

(*a*) ............................................................................................................

(*b*) ............................................................................................................

5   What is the most important economic factor in Corsica?

..............................................................................................................

B.  You decide to ring a French friend who lives in Lyon and whom you hope to visit on your way home. You suggest Saturday, 29th July as a possible day when you might call on him.
Listen to what he says and complete the question that follows in English in the space provided.

**6** For each of the dates given below write in what your friend is doing (one is already done for you by way of an example):

| | |
|---|---|
| 29 July | |
| 30 July | free all day |
| 31 July | |
| .............. | .................................................................. |
| 4 August | |

**C.** You are really enjoying your holiday and are thinking seriously about investing in a timeshare property in Corsica for future holidays. You go into an estate agency for details.

Listen to what the estate agent says and answer in English, in the spaces provided, the questions that follow.

**7** Complete the list of facilities on offer in the Marina di Santa Giulia for:

SWIMMING  (*a*) .....................................................................

(*b*) .....................................................................

BOATING  (*c*) .....................................................................

SHOPPING  (*d*) .....................................................................

(*e*) .....................................................................

(*f*) .....................................................................

(*g*) .....................................................................

**8** What special feature of the larger villas available is mentioned?

.................................................................................................................

**9** What special offer would be available to you during a visit to the Marina di Santa Giulia?

.................................................................................................................

**D.** You saw the sign below when you first arrived and have hired a television during your stay.

| **LOCATION TÉLÉVISEUR COULEUR: 105 F par semaine** |
|---|

You try to watch the news most evenings and one evening in particular the headlines are as follows on the tape.

Listen to the newsreader and answer in English in the spaces provided the questions that follow.

**10** How many were injured in the Paris incident?

...............................................................

**11** What two types of vehicle were involved in the Dijon accident?

(*a*) ...............................................

(*b*) ...............................................

**12** What is the likely suggested outcome of the dispute referred to in the third news item?

..................................................................................................

E. OPTIONAL WRITING (10 minutes extra)
Write your answer in French.

**13** While you are sitting out on the terrace of your villa, a young lady from the reception bureau in the holiday complex stops by, obviously in a hurry, asking after the people in the villa next to yours. Your neighbours are called Durand.

Listen to what she says. Since you are about to go out you write down the message in French so that you can leave it for your neighbours who are not in at the moment.

**Exercise 7**

THE LONDON CHAMBER OF COMMERCE EXAMINATIONS BOARD

FOREIGN LANGUAGES FOR INDUSTRY AND COMMERCE

FRENCH – ADVANCED – SECTION C         DIALOGUE A
                                      (Tape-recorded
                                      conversation)

Ecoutez attentivement la conversation qui suit. Après l'avoir écoutée, vous devez faire un résumé en anglais de cette conversation. Si vous le voulez, il vous est permis de prendre des notes.

*Conversation entre la secrétaire d'une compagnie d'assurances, Madame Chartier, et le propriétaire d'une usine, Monsieur Renault.*

# Part Six
## Answers to Exercises

Although every effort has been made to make the answers in this section as correct and relevant as possible, the various boards represented accept no responsibility for their accuracy.

# Answers to questions in Part One

## Reading

### Exercise A (pp. 11–13)

**1**

(a) Europe puts on a new skin.
(b) The ageing population of the countries of the northern hemisphere and possible consequences.

**2**

(a) En 2008, les pays du Nord ne représentent plus que 15% de l'humanité. Non seulement l'Europe se vide, mais encore elle vieillit. En France, dans 20 ans, les retraites devront être amputées de 30%. Le vide de l'Europe ne sera pas sans appeler des migrations. Des scénarios:
  - l'assimilation possible en cas de migration lente
  - les immigrants se constituent en groupes de pression – la haine raciale
  - l'éventualité optimiste – l'émergence d'une culture islamo-européenne

(b) The population of the countries in the North is ageing and shrinking – 50% of the world's population lived in the North in 1914, 25% in 1988. Within 20 years, Japan and Germany will have the oldest populations of any country.

The consequent drop in manpower will lead to mass immigration from the Third World, particularly from North Africa and the Middle East.

If immigration is slow and controlled, peaceful assimilation is possible; a rapid influx can cause racial conflict, violence and terrorism. Optimists look for the emergence of an Islamic-European culture.

3

(a)  Tripled.
(b)  1524 inhabitants per square kilometre.
(c)  more people over 60 than under 20.
(d)  Italy and Spain.

4

(a)  False; they are suggested alternatives.
(b)  True.
(c)  False; the President of Algeria.
(d)  False; octogenarians need people to look after them.

5
25 million
65 million
five
Asia Minor
slow
countries of origin
pressure
internal
foreign
diversity
mixed marriages
reciprocal

## Exercise B (pp. 14–15)
1

(a)  Expected revenue from the tunnel.
(b)  Share of cross-channel traffic – passengers and freight – taken by
     the tunnel.
(c)  The increase in passengers and freight crossing the Channel by the
     tunnel and the proportion carried by the shuttle as opposed to train.

2

(a)  1,000,000,000 F
(b)  8,730,000,000 F

3

(a)  109,700,000
(b)  41,300,000
(c)  191,600,000 tonnes
(d)  one-sixth

4

(a)  41,300,000
(b)  21,500,000
(c)  4,100,000

## Exercise C (pp. 15–17)
1

généralistes
tous
seulement/normalement/uniquement
justifiée
65%
régime
médicaments
psychologue/psychothérapiste
alimentation
enseignement

2

1%
80%
19%
46%

## Listening

## Exercise A (pp. 19–20)
1

(a)  Number of children killed or injured on the road.
(b)  5-plus.
(c)  Transport and Education.
(d)  Drivers and parents.
(e)  'Conduite' means driving and behaviour.
(f)  They trust their children on the road too quickly.

2

(a)  An Atlas.
(b)  22.
(c)  Quality of the maps, amount of statistical information, beauty of the illustrations.
(d)  On Tuesdays - fortnightly.
(e)  85 francs.

**Exercise B (pp. 20–21)**

1

(a) They are his greatest/best.

(b) Juvenile delinquency; children of broken marriages; colonialism.

(c) They are only the best in terms of sales figures.

(d) That all his works have high sales figures.

(e) None of them has sold many copies.

(f) Says he knows some people like him.

(g) Admits he is disliked by some/some see him as an enemy; feels disappointed; would prefer to be liked.

## Writing

**Exercise A (p. 28)**
See transcript (p. 216).

**Exercise B (p. 29)**
See transcript (p. 216).

**Exercise C (pp. 30–33).**
*N.B. For many of the questions there are no definitive answers, in which case those given below should be considered sound models.*

1

(a) Le rôle principal des vacances, c'est de vous faire vous relaxer.

(b) Ne pas rester trop longtemps à se bronzer en plein soleil.
Ne pas faire les achats pour les vacances à la dernière minute.
Ne pas manger la nourriture riche tous les jours.

(c) A mon avis, le conseil de ne pas faire d'excès quand on est en vacances est le plus important. Si on mange trop bien tous les jours, reste tous les soirs dans les boîtes jusqu'au petit matin, dort trop longtemps en plein soleil, la santé en souffre et les activités perdent de leur charme.

(d) Comment peut-on y aller et c'est à quelle distance?
Comment est l'hotel?
Qu'est-ce qu'on peut visiter dans la région?
Qu'est-ce qu'on peut faire comme sport?
Qu'est-ce qu'il y a comme distractions le soir?

2 Holidays have to change everything: wipe out the symptoms of stress, get rid of the strains of life. One Frenchman in two takes summer holidays of an average duration of twenty-five days, and by so doing, in normal circumstances, transforms the ordinary, sullen, exhausted, pale citizen into a tanned, confident, hearty

superman. But beware of traps! Innumerable summer holiday makers will come back in the same condition as they left. Even worse. Because they make many a blunder. They jostle each other in their thousands at the wheels of their cars all on the same day. They want to rest, but they wear themselves out by staying in night clubs until the early hours. They want to look good, and they lie down for hours at a stretch in the heat of the sun at the risk of 'leaving their skin behind.' They take care of their bodies, but exhaust themselves in physical activities for which nothing has prepared them. Taking advantage of a holiday is almost an art.

3

| | | |
|---|---|---|
| (a) réussir | (b) réseau | (c) partiez |
| (d) agacer | (e) venez | (f) que |
| (g) méfiez | (h) pourrait | (i) profiterez |
| (j) réglé | (k) de | (l) surménage |
| (m) à | (n) tranquille | |

4

(a) quand vous travailliez bien, vous obteniez l'approbation de vos collègues
(b) les ouvriers moins consciencieux que moi espéraient que je n'allais pas réussir
(c) ceux qui sont moins intelligents que moi
(d) ne lui permettaient pas de se mêler avec d'autres personnes
(e) qu'il trouvait partout à l'usine
(f) ma femme et moi étions toujours du même avis
(g) je n'avais pas été capable de bien faire mon travail

5   Jean et sa femme étaient mariés depuis cinq ans quand Maria est née. Lui-même, il supportait la haine de ceux qu'il méprisait, mais leurs procédés infâmes tourmentaient sa femme. A la fin elle est morte, et dès ce moment les voisins sans scrupules se sont mis à le harceler, lui et sa fille. Ses collègues jalousaient la réussite de Maria, dont l'avenir avait été assuré depuis qu'elle avait obtenu son avancement. Heureusement, elle et Jean sont restés indifférents à toute cette hostilité continuelle.

# Answers to questions in Part Two

## French for employment

### Exercise A (p. 52)

1   Petro-chemicals, aeronautics, transport.

2   No.

3   Market analysis, launching new products, drawing up and delivery of marketing plans, help with sales in France and Europe.

4   Practical knowledge of English, and ability to get on well with people, inspire others and work as a member of a team.

### Exercise B (pp. 53–54)
1
(a)   Commercial assistant.
(b)   Suppliers and customers.
(c)   Sales and stock control.

2
(a)   Abroad.
(b)   3-5 years.

3
(a)   Paris office.
(b)   Branch of an international company.

4   Pleasant and stable, speaks English.

# Answers to questions in Part Three

## Basic grammatical terms

### Exercise A (p. 61)
1
(a) millions, sportifs, substances, masse, force.
(b) International, Olympique, interdits.
(c) tenu, s'est agrandi.
(d) malheuresement, faire.

2
(a) le marché noir.
(b) anabolisants.
(c) masse musculaire.
(d) sportifs.
(e) interdits.

## Articles and nouns

### Exercise A (pp. 64–65)
1

| | |
|---|---|
| la voiture | the car |
| du luxe | luxury |
| du confort | comfort |
| de la vitesse | speed |
| l'Hirondelle | the Swallow |
| une moteur | an engine |
| (plus) de pannes | (no more) breakdowns |
| des freins | brakes |
| (plus) de soucis | (no more) worries |
| une ligne | a shape, line |
| (beaucoup) de coups d'oeil | (lots of) glances |
| un prix | a price |

2 Le vélo-moteur de votre choix. Vous voulez un moyen de transport simple sauf et bon marché. Le voilà! L'Aiglon a tout ce que vous désirez!

Une moteur économique (plus de grands comptes d'essence)
Des freins sûrs (plus de moments inquiétants)
Un cadre robuste et simple (plus de trucs chers)

Et tout ça à un prix raisonnable.

3 Une innovation, un plaisir, une mémoire, un témoin,
le rappel, l'indication, le goût, la recherche,
des notes, des lettres.

4

Découvrir un nouvel organisateur est toujours un plaisir rare. Notre mini-organisateur vous permet de dicter des notes et répondre aux lettres où et quand vous le décidez. Il vous offre une mémoire énorme, le rappel immédiat, l'indication de niveau des piles. Dans la recherche de perfection technologique, c'est un gagnant.

## Pronouns 1

### Exercise A (pp. 69–70)

| A | B |
|---|---|
| 1 | 4 |
| 2 | 6 |
| 3 | 1 |
| 4 | 7 |
| 5 | 2 |
| 6 | 5 |
| 7 | 3 |

## Pronouns 2

### Exercise A (pp. 72–73)
(a) le foie gras qui est …
(b) le foie gras qu'on a examiné …
(c) le foie gras dont on parle vient …
(d) les blocs de foie dans lesquels ils ont trouvé …
(e) le producteur accusé à qui ils ont parlé …

### Exercise B (p. 74)
(a) Qu'est-ce que la Côte d'Azur possède? *or*
Que possède la Côte d'Azur?

(b) Qui y sont attirés?
(c) Qu'est-ce que la région offre aux visiteurs? *or*
    Qu'offre la région aux visiteurs?
(d) Pour qui est-ce que la Côte d'Azur change d'image?
(e) Lequel de ces changements aimez-vous le mieux?

**Exercise C (pp. 74–75)**
1

(a) bonbons
(b) vélo
(c) voiture
(d) idées

2

(a) our sweets
(b) a bike
(c) my car
(d) ideas

**Exercise D (p. 76)**

| | | |
|---|---|---|
| tu | you | subject |
| le tien | yours | possessive |
| c' | it | subject |
| celui que | the one which | demonstrative |
| moi | me | disjunctive |
| Qui | who | interrogative |
| t' | you | indirect object |
| m' | me | indirect object |
| celui-ci | this one | demonstrative |
| le mien | mine | possessive |
| toi | you | disjunctive |
| Que | what | interrogative |
| tu | you | subject |
| lequel | which one | interrogative |
| à moi | mine | possessive/ disjunctive |

## Adjectives

**Exercise A (p. 80)**

étroites, autres, immenses, accumulée, différents, technologiques, grande

**Exercise B (p. 81)**

défavorables, ses (pneus), meilleure, toutes, ses (systemes), novatrice, vantés, ajoutés, intégrale, permanente, perfectionnée.

## Adverbs and prepositions

**Exercise A (pp. 85–86)**

2

passionnément, follement, tendrement, dévouement, désespérément, éternellement, toujours, difficilement

**Exercise B (p. 87)**

1

de, vers, avec, dans, de, sous, de, à, de derrière.

2

Jojo court vers son trou, mais Tom lui barre le chemin. Tom chasse Jojo trois fois autour de la table. Jojo court sous le canapé, le long du radiateur, sur la table, derrière une chaise et retrouve enfin son trou.

**Exercise C (p. 89)**

1

à, sans, jusqu'à, sur, à, A, derrière, Au-dessus des, à, tout près de, au-dessous de, A, de, à, à, à, sans, aux

2

We take off from Dubai and climb smoothly to 10,000 metres. Outside the air flows over the 'plane at an incredible speed. At 4.15 a.m. dawn breaks. The rising sun is behind us. Above the Alps we run into a thunder storm. A flash of lightning illuminates the clouds near the plane, but the danger passes and soon the sun returns. The Thames appears below us. At 9.25 a.m. we are approaching Heathrow, where we are due to land at 9.30 a.m. The 'plane begins its descent and we prepare to leave, with no thought of the perils of the night.

## Verbs 1

**Exercise A (p. 95)**

1

Tu ignores ... je suis le premier chimiste industriel ... je ne parle jamais de mes recherches ... je remporte ... peux-tu ... mon nom.

2

Ils sont ... adolescents ... Ils ne savent ... Ils font ... Ils portent ... ils chantent ... Ils ne choisissent pas leur chemin ... Ils suivent leur chef ... Ils attendent ... ils arrivent ... ils hurlent leur slogan.

### Exercise B (p. 98)

1

saura ... obtiendra ... remportera ... sera ... devra-t-il ... dépendra ... se tromperont.

2

Next Sunday the final result of the general election will be known. Is the Socialist party going to obtain an absolute majority of the seats or will the Right be victorious? What will be the situation with regard to the President? Is he going to have to try to form a coalition or a kind of national union? All will depend on the complicated voting system in France. What is certain is that, once again, the opinion polls will be mistaken.

### Exercise C (p. 100–101)

1

envoya ... resta ... conduisit ... écrivit ... jeta ... prit ... montra ... le laissa ... mourut ... l'enterra.

2

(a) The castle on L'Ile Marguerite.
(b) 29 years.
(c) The Bastille.
(d) On a plate thrown out of the window.
(e) He could not read.

## Verbs 2

### Exercise A (p. 104)

portait ... datait ... laissait ... était ... avait ... souriait ... faisait ... s'illuminait ... avait ... avait ... regardait ... passaient ... jouaient ... séparait.

### Exercise B (pp. 106–107)

1

serait ... ne serait pas ... s'opposerait ... seraient ... devrions ... auraient ... attendait ... aiderait.

2

(a) Should be based on socialist principles.
(b) French social gains would be lost through the influence of capitalist market forces.
(c) Discussions between companies and trade unions of multinationals on a European scale would have to be started to combat unemployment.

## Verbs 3

### Exercise A (p. 111)

1

me suis levée ... j'ai attrapé ... est arrivé ... ont commencé ... j'ai eu ... j'ai mangé ... n'avais que ... j'ai retrouvé ... ont duré ... n'ai pas regardé ... il n'y avait pas ... suis montée ... j'ai mis ... me suis couchée.

### Exercise B (p. 114)

1

aurez suivi ... avait lu ... expliquait ... j'aurais voulu ... fut sorti

2

(a) 'Vous auriez été plus motivé(s) si vous aviez suivi un stage des arts martiaux.'
(b) 'J'avais voulu apprendre le kendo.'
(c) Quand il eut lu le livre, il sortit.

## Verbs 4

### Exercise A (pp. 117–118)

1

(a) 7 rester, discuter, protéger, persuader, limiter, détruire, payer.
(b) 4 ayant, disant, attaquant, affirmant.
(c) 3 protéger, détruire, persuader (possible)
(d) 4 pour discuter, de protéger, de nous persuader, en train de détruire.
(e) 4 rester, persuader, limiter, payer.

### Exercise B (p. 119)

1

Imagine ... tu es ... Découvre ... Allonge-toi ... Mets ... nage ... Goûte ... mange ... bois ... Cherche-le ... Trouve-le ... Cache-toi ... Viens ... amuse-toi ... Dépêche-toi ... t'attendent.

2

Ne mange pas les fruits de mer! Ne bois pas le vin de la région! Le passé? Ne le cherche pas dans les villages! Ne te cache pas dans le sien de la nature, mais vas-y et amuse-toi bien!

**Verbs 5**

**Exercise A (p. 122)**

The number of computer crimes increases yearly. Alarming figures of more than 100 per day *have been revealed* by a recent enquiry. Ten years ago, only the administration and management of a company *were put* on computer records. Today, all the essential activities *are put* on disc. The heart of a company, it's information, *is found* in the computer. Commercial battles *will no longer be won* except by ensuring the security of this information.

Sometimes security is minimal – discs *are kept* in a cupboard, the whereabouts of whose key is common knowledge. People are often unaware, however, of the real threat, human intervention. Many of these criminals *are found* in the company itself. A virus, which develops in the same way as certain physical ailments, can *be introduced*. Most French financial institutions *have been affected* by automatic fraud. In America the Mafia *was called to mind* and it *is postulated* that the 'crash' of '87 *was caused* by an attack (a virus perhaps) on the Wall Street computer system.

(The passives in the passage are in italics).

**Exercise B (pp. 129)**
1

(a)  ... puisse ...
(b)  ... consiste ...
(c)  ... nous abandonnions ...
(d)  ... ne devienne ...
(e)  ... sachent ...
(f)  ... soit ...

2

(a)  ... le projet le plus audace qui ait capturé ...

**Helpful hints**

**Exercise B (p. 134)**

Between 1985 and 1987 from 110,000 to 120,000 jobs were lost per annum. There were more than 2,000,000 people unemployed. Industrial investment this year progressed from 11% to 12% and manufactured exports rose 7% in output. It is hoped that this is the end of the decline in the rundown of the country's industry.

## Exercise C (p. 137)

| Present | Future *(je)* | Past Historic *(je)* | Past Participle |
|---|---|---|---|
| J'écris | écrirai | écrivis | écrit |
| Tu écris | | | |
| Il écrit | | | |
| Nous écrivons | | | |
| Vous écrivez | | | |
| Ils écrivent | | | |
| Je prends | prendrai | pris | pris |
| Tu prends | | | |
| Il prend | | | |
| Nous prenons | | | |
| Vous prenez | | | |
| Ils prennent | | | |
| Je vois | verrai | vis | vu |
| Tu vois | | | |
| Il voit | | | |
| Nous voyons | | | |
| Vous voyez | | | |
| Ils voient | | | |
| Je reçois | recevrai | reçus | reçu |
| Tu reçois | | | |
| Il reçoit | | | |
| Nous recevons | | | |
| Vous recevez | | | |
| Ils reçoivent | | | |

## Exercise D (p. 138)

tu vas … nouvelle … était … partir … apporte … tu seras … tu verras … n'oublie pas … trouver … achetées … était … bonne … entra … répondit … confus … l'ai … oublié.

# Answers to questions in Part Five

### Exercise 1 (p. 153)

(a) flooding
new forms of cancer
increase in carbon gases in atmosphere
(b) soil erosion
(c) urgent coordinated action required
(d) les glaces polaires fondront
(e) une bonne partie de nos territoires sera inondée
(f) les rayons ultra-violets du soleil provoqueraient des cancers nouveaux
(g) il y aura un accroissement rapide du taux du gaz carbonique

### Exercise 2 (pp. 154–155)

(a) (i)    43.25.43.98.
   (ii)   November – April
  (iii)  6 weeks

(b) (i)    11 – 18
   (ii)   20 years

(c) (i)    Maths, Physics, French, English, German, Spanish
   (ii)   All Saints, Christmas, February, Easter, Summer

(d) (i)    P à D
   (ii)   individual

(e) (i)    A B C D
   (ii)   900 – 1200 F per subject

(f) (i)    Catch up and support
   (ii)   Monday – Saturday

(g) (i)    private lessons at home
   (ii)   intensive courses in Paris and suburbs

**Exercise 3 (pp. 155–157)**

(b)  Specimen curriculum vitae

| | |
|---|---|
| Nom: | Brown |
| Prénom: | John |
| Adresse: | 1,Oxford Road, Rugby CV6 0JH |
| Age: | 29 ans |
| Date de Naissance: | 6 juin 19– |
| Sexe: | Mâle (célibataire) |
| Nationalité: | Britannique |
| Profession: | Vendeur |
| Lieu de Travail: | Evans and Co., Tile Industrial Estate, Coventry |
| Expérience Professionelle: | 1988–91: Journaliste (Service des Ventes) Worksop News. 1991 jusqu'au présent. Directeur des Ventes, Evans and Co. |
| Diplômes: | A Levels – Mathematiques, Français, Anglais Diplôme en Communications et Informatique, Liverpool Polytechnic |
| Stage: | Formation en Marketing, Wolverhampton Polytechnic |
| Langues: | Courant en français, comprend et parle allemand |
| Disponibilité: | un mois |
| Intérêts: | Voyager, langues, le ski |

**Exercise 4 (pp. 157–160)**

**Assessment check-list**

A:  CONTENU

La lettre doit contenir le suivant:

1    Un remerciement à M. Dahni pour sa lettre
2    Qualité – les mèches ne sont point inférieures à celles des Allemands
3    Prix – quel est le prix maximum qu'on puisse demander pour rester toujours en concurrence avec les Italiens?
4    Dates – quelles sont les dates précises du passage de M. Dahni en Algérie pour qu'on puisse informer ENCIDEX par telex?
5    La Tunisie – il y a six tôleries sur la liste de M. Dahni. Quelles sont les quatre qu'il faut contacter?
6    Le Maroc – oui, on peut envoyer un échantillon de mèches, mais à Marseille ou au Maroc direct? S'il faut passer par Marseille, sera-t-on censé de payer les droits de douane deux fois: en France et en Afrique?

7   Contrat – les notaires ont presque fini de rédiger le contrat qui doit arriver chez lui au début de la semaine prochaine pour sa signature

B:  STYLE

1   Style correct, pas de mots familiers

2   La lettre doit commencer correctement – 'Cher Monsieur Dahni', pas 'Mon cher Dahni'

3   Elle doit terminer avec une des formules convenables – 'veuillez agréer', etc

4   Avant la formule terminale il faut avoir une phrase pour achever convenablement – 'dans l'attente de votre réponse'

### Exercise 5 (pp. 161–176)

### Assessment check-list

(Numbers i–v refer to points requested in candidate's task brief)

i)   Bison Futé is an operation (its logo being a red Indian – Crafty Bison) mounted by the French Transport Ministry each year to help the motorist in the following ways:

(a) gives information about days for going on or coming back from holiday when traffic is likely to be heavy and which therefore should be avoided if possible
     red days – very heavy
     orange days – quite heavy

(b) gives information about best times for travelling in order to avoid dense traffic on days of heavy traffic flow

(c) sets up centres that the motorist can telephone to get information about road conditions

(d) sets up green signs showing alternative routes that will avoid the main traffic flow

(e) sets up yellow signs on motorways or their approach roads saying that the motorway is choked with traffic

(f) persuades big petrol companies to keep some of their petrol stations open during the night

(g) sets up on main roads reception areas where the motorist can get information about traffic conditions or general tourist information.

ii)  It gives dates, times and places of expected heavy traffic flow, including traffic jams and roadworks on main roads and motorways.

iii) (a) It is quicker to take the motorway even when it is jammed than to do the extra miles on the alternative routes

(b) the added journey length of the alternative routes leads to fatigue and is therefore dangerous

(c)  alternative routes are not adapted to holiday traffic – narrow roads, no proper signposting, not many petrol stations open at night

*but*

(d)  motorway is more expensive

(e)  alternative routes are more picturesque – fine when you want to take your time.

iv)  (a)  A controversy within the EC about yellow or white headlights:
   white only – Germany
   yellow only – France
   either allowed – elsewhere

  (b)  EC directive states that they can be either but the directive only applies where a country does not have contrary pre-existing legislation

  (c)  no governmental moves at the moment to clarify issue.

v)  Although white headlights are against the law on French cars in France, they are allowed on foreign cars in France.

(Note: The law has now changed to make it legal for French cars to have white headlights.)

## Exercise 6: Part 1 (pp. 177–182)

1

(a)  long stretches of sand

(b)  small bays of sand and rocks

(c)  unspoilt beaches

(d)  limestone cliffs

2

(a)  eagles, trout

(b)  wild boar

3

(b)  trout streams

(c)  lakes, snow capped peaks

4

(a)  advised to book

(b)  reduction on most hotels

5  furnished rural holidays homes to let

6  accommodation is bed and breakfast only; this type of accommodation is not yet widely available in Corsica

7

(a)  a threat to beauty spots

(b)  forbidden on the coast, owner's permission necessary

8

(a) meals can be provided
(b) facilities for self catering available

9

(a) keep your distance
(b) only use hard shoulder in emergencies

10

(a) take notice of warnings, never bathe alone
(b) do not let them out of your sight
(c) wear a harness, life jacket and wet suit

11

(a) distress rocket
(b) torch

12

(a) listen to weather forecasts
(b) tell someone where you are going, the number in the group and
the time of return, go with experienced people

13  do not destroy vegetation, leave litter, light fires

## Exercise 6: Part 2 (pp. 183–185)

*R.S.A.   Level 2   Part 2   Listening Skills.*

1
170 = distance in kilometres from France
 83 = distance in kilometres from Italy
180 = length in kilometres of island
 80 = width in kilometres of island

2

(a) water always pleasantly warm
(b) unpolluted

3

(a) sailing, windsurfing
(b) water skiing, fishing, under-water diving

4

(a) used to be a hiding place for bandits
(b) sheep rearing

5  tourism

6

29 July going to niece's wedding
31 July holidays begin
 4 August leaving for Switzerland

7

(a)  large heated swimming pool
(b)  with restaurant and bar
(c)  port for pleasure craft
(d)  supermarket
(e)  bakers-confectioners
(f)  butchers
(g)  tobacconist-newsagents

8  have gardens

9  free dinner

10  none

11

(a)  lorry
(b)  coach

12  strike

13  M.Durand allez vite à la réception. Votre frère a téléphoné de Paris.
    Votre mère est malade et on l'a transportée à l'hôpital. La réception
    a tous les détails.

## Exercise 7 (p. 185)

M.Renault, an industrialist, who has just had a factory built on the
outskirts of the town, is enquiring about insurance for the factory. He
wants cover for fire, theft and public liability.

Building cover will be assessed by the valuation of the insurance
company's surveyor, not through the invoices submitted by M.Renault.

The insurance company needs to know what products are manufactured and the storage area before assessing cover for contents, raw
materials and machinery.

The factory produces kitchen furniture made from solid oak, Nor-
wegian pine, veneered oak and white wood. The warehouse is 2000
square metres in area.

Because of the considerable fire risk, cover against fire would be 10
per cent above normal. M.Renault objects to this since smoking is
forbidden and all buildings are protected by smoke detectors and
extinguishers.

Cover against theft however, can be reduced by 20 per cent for the first year and 28 per cent for the second year (providing there are no claims) since the factory will have its own 24-hour guard on site, who will be replaced by a guard from a security firm during holidays.

Public liability can be set at 500 million francs since the work force is less than 100.

If M.Renault insured his lorries through the company, the premium would be reduced by a third. Cover would be on a yearly basis renewable on the 31st December. Two months notice is required to cancel. The surveyor will call within the next two days. M.Renault leaves his telephone number.

# Part Seven
Transcript of Tape

# Transcript of tape

## Chapter 1

### Artists in Paris

Combien d'étudiants y a-t-il?
En quoi consiste le cours?
Pourquoi étudiez-vous les Impressionistes?
Vous avez vu des peintures des Impressionistes?
Où?
Qu'est-ce que vous avez fait à Montmartre?
Pourquoi est-ce que Monmartre est un quartier préféré des peintres?
Vous allez visiter d'autres endroits?
Lesquels?
L'invention de l'appareil photographique a beaucoup influencé les peintres du dix-neuvième siècle. Laquelle préférez-vous, une belle photo ou une mauvaise peinture?
Pourquoi?

### Radio: la musique plus que l'information

Est-ce que les jeunes de neuf ans écoutent la radio plus fréquemment que les jeunes de quinze ans?
Combien d'heures par semaine est-ce que les étudiants écoutent la radio?
Quelles sont les radios préférées des jeunes?
Quel pourcentage d'étudiants écoute les radios locales?
Pourquoi les jeunes, écoutent-ils la radio?
Quelles émissions est-ce qu'ils préfèrent?
Et les adultes, à quoi s'intéressent-ils?
Quelle sorte de musique est écoutée le plus souvent?
Quel âge ont les gens qui écoutent le plus fréquemment les chansons?
la musique rock?
la grande musique?
Ecoutez-vous souvent la radio?

Quand?
Quelles émissions préférez-vous?
Préférez-vous les actualités à la radio, ou à la télé?
Pourquoi?
Quels sont les avantages de la radio sur la télé?

## Les grandes surfaces

Je préfère faire mes achats dans les grandes surfaces. C'est plus pratique, plus facile, surtout si on travaille. On peut tout acheter au même endroit et profiter d'heures d'ouverture plus longues. Il y a toute une gamme de produits, y compris les vêtements, les produits électro-ménagers. Toute la famille peut y aller faire les courses et s'amuser en même temps. Il faut être prudent et je fais une liste pour éviter d'acheter plus que je n'ai besoin. Et le parking, pas de problème.

## Description

Les femmes, où sont-elles?
Comment sont-elles?
Qu'est-ce qu'elles font?
Qu'est-ce qu'elles disent?
Elles sont contentes. Pour quelle raison, pensez-vous?
A votre avis, quelle est leur profession?
La dame qui porte les bouteilles, qui est-elle?
Décrivez le monsieur qui les regarde.
Qu'est-ce qu'il pense d'elles?

## Chapter 3

Extract No 1

Lancement aujourd'hui d'une campagne pour faire baisser le nombre d'enfants qui sont tués chaque année ou gravement blessés dans les accidents de la route. C'est la première cause de mortalité des enfants qui ont plus de cinq ans. Le Ministre des Transports et son collègue le Ministre de l'Education vont présenter aujourd'hui le slogan de leur campagne . . . 'Choisissons la vie, changeons de conduite.' Cela s'adresse aux automobilistes, bien sûr, mais également aux parents qui ont parfois tendance à faire trop vite confiance à leurs enfants.

Extract No 2

Innovation spectaculaire! Voici le grand Atlas de la France . . . chez tous les marchands de journaux . . . édité en 22 luxueux volumes grand format. Le grand Atlas de la France n'a pas son pareil pour la qualité de cartographie, l'abondance des renseignements statistiques, la beauté des illustrations et des photos ... le grand Atlas de la France ... vendu un mardi sur deux ... chaque exemplaire prévoyez 85 francs.

*Troisième partie*
Dans cette partie vous allez entendre une interview entre un reporter et un écrivain. A la fin, vous étudierez les questions et vous écrirez des notes. Ensuite vous entendrez l'interview une deuxième fois; cette fois vous pourrez prendre des notes en écoutant. Puis vous aurez sept minutes pour rédiger vos réponses.

R: Gilbert Cesbron, il y a trente-trois livres dans votre oeuvre. On connaît les grands, il y a *Chiens perdus sans collier, Les Saints vont en enfer* et au théâtre il y a *Il est minuit docteur Schweitzer*. Il y a toujours dans ce que vous écrivez ...

C: C'étaient les titres qui ont font la joie des chansonniers.

R: Oui, mais il faut aller au-delà de ces titres, car les thèmes traités, c'est la délinquance juvénile, c'est les enfants du divorce, c'est le colonialisme avec *Il est minuit* ...

C: Oui, enfin c'est autre chose ... vous avez dit que ce sont les grands livres. C'est bien de l'honneur, mais c'était là peut-être une question de tirage, c'est-à-dire du nombre vendu.

R: Oui, ils ont eu de grands tirages, ceux-là. De toute manière, vous avez toujours de grands tirages.

C: Non, pas de tout, détrompez-vous, détrompez-vous. J'ai publié trente-trois livres, sur ces trentes-trois il y a quinze romans. Or, c'est seulement les romans qui ont eu du succès. Mon dernier livre est le quinzième roman.

R: Qui s'appelle *Voici le temps des imposteurs*, n'est-ce pas?

C: Oui, c'est le numéro quinze des romans.

R: Mais les autres livres, qu'est-ce que c'est?

C: Les autres livres, c'est du théâtre, précisément, ou des essais, ou des contes, et alors là, il n'y a pas du tout, du tout, de grands tirages, ce sont de ...

R: Oui, mais vous avez votre public, Gilbert Cesbron.

C: Il y a des gens qui m'aiment bien.

R: Et vous provoquez aussi parfois l'hostilité.

C: Oui, là, là, sûrement, et je suis un imbécile, car ça me fait de la peine, c'est très bête, mais moi, je n'ai pas d'ennemis – je n'ai pas d'ennemis à moi, je veux dire, mais je suis l'ennemi d'un certain nombre de gens et chaque fois ça me fait de la peine. Oui, c'est idiot, je voudrais être aimé, on est tous comme ça.

Lisez les questions numéros 'a' à 'g'. Vous avez sept minutes pour écrire des notes. (Stop the tape recorder for this length of time.)

Voici l'interview pour la deuxième fois. Vous pouvez prendre des notes en écoutant.

2nd reading

Vous avez sept minutes pour rédiger vos réponses.
(7 minutes)

## Chapter 4

*Le Champagne*
La région de Champagne est une très ancienne province de France située à environ 150 kilomètres au nord-est de Paris. La température annuelle moyenne de la Champagne ne dépasse pas 10,5°C. Trois cépages sont parfaitement adaptés au sol et au climat de la Champagne – le Pinot Noir, le Meunier et le Chardonnay.

Après les vendanges, faites à la main, les moûts sont logés dans les cuves pour la première fermentation qui transformera, en quelques semaines, le jus du raisin en vin. Lorsque la cuvée est composée, on ajoute une petite quantité de sucre de canne et de ferment et le vin est mis en bouteilles, bouché, puis couché sur 'lattes' dans les caves obsures et fraîches de la Champagne. La lente transformation du sucre, sous l'effet des ferments, suscite la prise de la mousse. On laisse les bouteilles plusieurs années en cave.

La seconde fermentation provoque la formation d'un dépôt dans la bouteille. La technique champenoise permet d'éliminer le dépôt en conservant le vin dans sa bouteille. On ajoute ensuite la liqueur de dosage qui détermine le type de vin recherché (brut, sec, demi-sec). La bouteille reçoit enfin son bouchon définitif et l'étiquette.

Pour apprécier le champagne il faut:
garder les bouteilles couchées à l'horizontale
servir le champagne frais, mais non glacé
utiliser des verres en forme de tulipe ou de flûte.

## Dictation
Créée en 1973,/la compagnie 'Taureau'/a rejoint le groupe Smith/ en 1990./Forte de son enracinement/dans l'assurance traditionelle en France,/elle a ainsi,/avec enthousiasme,/enrichi son expérience/des nouvelles capacités/apportées par la puissance/d'un groupe international./A la gamme des métiers classiques/de la prévoyance collective/elle a ajouté/de nouvelles formules d'assurance./La compagnie continuera/à tous moments/de défendre vos intérêts.

## Translation
Founded in 1973,/the company 'Taureau'/joined the Smith group/in 1990./Strongly rooted/in traditional insurance in France,/it thus,/en-

thusiastically,/increased its experience/with the new capabilities/brought through the strength/of an international group./To the range of classical areas/of collective insurance/it added new types of insurance./The company will continue/at all times/to serve your interests.

## Extra practice

### Exercise 6: Part 2
A. *Welcome guide at holiday complex (female)*

Tout d'abord je voudrais vous présenter la Corse.

Située à cent soixante-dix kilomètres de la France et à quatre-vingt-trois kilomètres de l'Italie, la Corse est une des trois grandes îles de la Méditerranée. Elle fait, à peu près, cent quatre-vingts kilomètres de long et quatre-vingts kilomètres de large.

Il y a, si vous voulez, deux Corses: la Corse de la mer et la Corse des montagnes.

La Corse de la mer est la Corse touristique. La température de la mer est toujours agréable, même en hiver, et la qualité des eaux est exceptionnelle. On peut pratiquer de nombreuses activités nautiques, par exemple, la voile, la planche à voile, le ski nautique, la pêche, la plongée sous-marine.

L'intérieur est célèbre pour ses montagnes, qui étaient dans le passé le refuge des bandits, et qui maintenant sont l'habitat des moutons.

Le climat est chaud et sec en été, et doux en hiver. Dans les vallées on produit surtout des fruits — pommes, poires, abricots, cerises, pêches, raisins. C'est une ressource importante pour l'île mais c'est surtout le tourisme qui domine l'économie aujourd'hui.

La Corse est française depuis ...

B. *Friend on telephone (male)*

Samedi, tu as dit, le vingt-neuf? Non, ce n'est pas possible. On est invité au mariage de ma nièce. Mais dimanche, le trente, ça peut aller. Nous serons libres. Tu pourras aussi rester deux ou trois jours parce que mes vacances commencent le lundi, le trente et un juillet. Nous allons en Suisse mais on part le 4 août. Ça t'arrange?

C. *Estate agent (female)*

Bon, alors, la Marina di Santa Giulia est un village de vacances dans la Corse du Sud, à seize kilomètres de Porto Vecchio. Il y a le village, bien sûr, la plage, un port de plaisance et un centre commercial avec supermarché, boulangerie-pâtisserie, boucherie, tabac-journaux. Dans le coeur du village il y a une grande piscine chauffée avec un restaurant et un bar. Il y a aussi deux courts de tennis et un minigolf.

On peut à présent vous offrir deux types de villa. Il y a des deux pièces avec terrasse plus cuisine et salle de douche/wc. Et des quatres pièces avec un grand jardin privé. Toutes les villas sont, bien sûr, meublées et très bien équipées.

Si vous voulez visiter la Marina aujourd'hui, par exemple, je peux tout organiser. Taxi à quatre heures cet après-midi, visite de la Marina, on vous offrira le dîner, absolument gratuit, dans le restaurant à côté de la piscine et vous serez de retour chez vous vers neuf heures ce soir. Ça vous intéresse?

D.   *TV newsreader (male)*

Attentat à la bombe à l'aéroport Charles de Gaulle, à Paris ce matin. Heureusement pas de blessés. Deux suspects sont à présent questionnés par la police.

Accident dramatique sur l'autoroute A6 près de Dijon. Heurté par un camion, un autocar rempli de touristes belges quitte la chaussée et s'enforce dans un canal. Il y aurait 32 morts.

Services des car-ferrys entre la France et la Grande Bretagne de nouveau menacés. Une dispute a éclaté entre les employés et la direction de Sealink. La grève, est-elle inévitable? Reportage de notre envoyé spécial, à Douvres.

E.   *Employee (female) from holiday village reception bureau*

Ah, bonjour, vous avez vu Monsieur Durand? Non? Bon, alors, si vous le voyez, pourrez-vous lui transmettre un message, s'il vous plaît? C'est très urgent. Voilà. Monsieur Durand doit passer à la réception immédiatement. Son frère a téléphoné ce matin, de Paris. Il a dit que leur mère était malade et qu'elle était à l'hôpital. Tous les détails sont à la réception. Merci beaucoup.

## Exercise 7

| | |
|---|---|
| Mme Chartier: | Bonjour monsieur, que désirez-vous? |
| M. Renault: | Bonjour madame. Je viens de faire construire une usine dans les environs de votre ville et je voudrais savoir quels sont vos conditions et tarifs d'assurance. |
| Mme C: | Oui, très bien. Alors, quels sont les risques que vous voulez couvrir? |
| M. R: | D'abord l'incendie, ensuite le vol, et enfin la responsabilité civile. |
| Mme C: | Bon. Pour établir le montant de votre prime incendie, il va falloir que je sache exactement la valeur des bâtiments de votre usine. |
| M. R: | Je peux vous transmettre les factures de mon architecte et de mon entrepreneur. |

| | |
|---|---|
| Mme C: | Ce serait utile mais il faut vous envoyer notre expert, pour qu'il nous donne son estimation personnelle. |
| M. R: | Bien entendu! |
| Mme C: | Il vous faudra une assurance différente pour couvrir le contenu, comme les matières premières, les machines ... Il faut donc que je sache ce que vous manufacturez et quelle est la superficie des locaux où vous entreposez la marchandise en instance de livraison. |
| M. R: | Nous fabriquons des meubles de cuisine, à des prix très variés, selon la matière première utilisée. Cela va du chêne massif au bois mélaminé, en passant par le sapin de Norvège, le plaqué chêne et le bois blanc. Nos entrepôts couvrent une superficie de 2000 mètres carrés. |
| Mme C: | Les risques d'incendie sont considérables. Il faudra compter une majoration de 10 pour cent sur nos tarifs normaux. |
| M. R: | Cela me semble un peu dur! Nous prenons toutes les précautions nécessaires. Il est naturellement absolument interdit de fumer dans les ateliers ainsi que dans les entrepôts. Tous les bâtiments sont munis de détecteurs de fumée et d'extincteurs. Enfin, venons-en au vol. |
| Mme C: | Pour couvrir le vol, il me faut savoir si votre usine sera gardée pendant la nuit et pendant les congés. |
| M. R: | J'ai l'intention d'avoir sur place un employé qui sera chargé de la surveillance nuit et jour, toute l'année, excepté pendant les congés annuels où il sera remplacé par un membre d'une société spécialisée dans les gardiennages d'usine. |
| Mme C: | Cela nous permettra de réduire votre prime de 20 pour cent pour la première année et de 28 pour cent pour la seconde, à la condition qu'il n'y ait pas de sinistre. |
| M. R: | Parfait. Et en ce qui concerne la responsabilité civile? |
| Mme. C: | Nous pouvons vous assurer pour la somme de 500 millions de francs, si le nombre de vos employés ne dépasse pas la centaine. |
| M. R: | J'aurai 75 ouvriers dans les ateliers et une dizaine d'employés dans les bureaux. |
| Mme C: | Cela ne pose donc aucun problème. |
| M. R: | Si mes camions étaient assurés par vous, me consentiriez-vous un tarif avantageux? |
| Mme C: | Bien sûr, si nous couvrons tout votre matériel de transport, nous pouvons réduire votre prime d'assurance d'un tiers. |

| | |
|---|---|
| M. R: | Tout cela me semble satisfaisant. |
| Mme C: | J'ajoute que, après la première période d'assurance, qui s'étend de la date de prise d'effet du contrat au 31 décembre, l'année d'assurance commence le premier janvier et s'achève le 31 décembre, date à laquelle sont dûes les cotisations. |
| M. R: | Et si je veux résilier mon contrat? |
| Mme C: | C'est très facile, mais il faut un préavis de deux mois. |
| M. R: | Eh bien, j'attends votre expert. Le plus tôt sera le mieux. |
| Mme C: | Je lui demanderai de vous téléphoner pour prendre rendez-vous. |
| M. R: | Mon numéro de téléphone est 1-397 54 43. |
| Mme C: | Très bien. Il se mettra en rapport avec vous demain ou après-demain au plus tard. |
| M. R: | D'accord. Au revoir, madame, et merci. |
| Mme C: | Je vous en prie. Au revoir, monsieur. |

# Part Eight
Vocabulary

# Vocabulary

## A

| | |
|---|---|
| accoutrement (m) | equipment |
| accroissement (m) | increase |
| accueillir | to greet |
| achats(m pl) | shopping |
| s'acheminer | to progress |
| acquis (m) | attainment |
| actualités (f pl) | news |
| affirmer | to assert |
| afflux (m) | rush |
| agir | to act |
| aiguille (f) | needle |
| aiguiller | to switch to |
| aimant (m) | magnet |
| amaigrissement (m) | slimming |
| aménagé | equipped |
| '(à l') appareil' | 'speaking' (*when answering telephone*) |
| approche (f) | approach |
| armateur (m) | shipowner |
| astre (m) | star |
| atout (m) | trump |
| atteindre | to reach |
| atterrir | to land |
| augmenter | to increase |
| autel (m) | altar |
| avarié | rotten |

| | |
|---|---|
| avenir (m) | future |
| avis (m) | opinion |
| avoir conscience | to be aware |
| avoir cours | to be current |

## B

| | |
|---|---|
| banlieue (f) | suburbs |
| (au) bas mot | at the lowest estimate |
| batelier (m) | boatman |
| bête (adj) | foolish |
| bévue (f) | blunder |
| blafard | pale |
| boîte de nuit (f) | night club |
| bonne bouffe (f) | large meal |
| se borner | to be limited to |
| boucher | to cork |
| boue (f) | mud |
| boulot (m) | work |
| bourdon (m) | drone |
| bourrer le crâne | to stuff your head |
| brise-glace (m) | ice-breaker |
| broche (f) | spit |

## C

| | |
|---|---|
| cadre (m) | framework, office manager |
| calcaire (adj) | limestone |
| carence (f) | deficiency |
| carmin | blood red |
| cataclysme (m) | disaster |
| céder | to give way to |
| cépage (m) | vine plant |
| chalandière (f) | punt |
| chandail (m) | sweater |
| chansonnier (m) | song writer |
| char (m) | tank or armoured vehicle |
| cheoir (OF) | to fall |
| chiffre (m) | figure |
| chômage (m) | unemployment |
| compétivité (f) | competitiveness |
| conduite (f) | driving, behaviour |
| consommation (f) | consumption |
| conte (m) | short story |
| convenable | suitable |
| coquillage (m) | shellfish |
| cortège (m) | procession |

| | |
|---|---|
| cotisation (f) | contribution |
| coupable | guilty |
| couramment | fluently |
| coureur de mer (m) | sea farer |
| courrier de dépêches (m) | dispatch messenger |
| crainte (f) | fear |
| crocheteur (m) | street porter |
| cueillir | to gather |
| curée (f) | quarry |
| cuve (f) | vat |

## D

| | |
|---|---|
| déchet (m) | waste product |
| décoller | to take off |
| dédale (m) | maze |
| se défoncer | to wear oneself out |
| se dégager | to be emitted |
| dégrader | to damage |
| délinquance juvenile (f) | juvenile delinquence |
| délirant | frantic |
| (sur) demande | (on) request |
| démenti (m) | contradiction |
| dénouer | to untie |
| déprime (f) | depression |
| derviche (m) | dervish |
| desclose (OF) | opened |
| désespoir (m) | despair (m) |
| se détendre | to relax |
| détrompez-vous! | don't you believe it! |
| digue (f) | breakwater |
| dispos | hearty |
| dodo (m *slang*) | sleep |
| don (m) | gift |
| douteux | doubtful |
| draguer | to dredge |
| drogue (f) | drug |

## E

| | |
|---|---|
| éblouir | to dazzle |
| éclair (m) | flash of lightning |
| s'éclater | to wear oneself out |
| effacer | to wipe out |
| effet de serre (m) | greenhouse effect |
| efficace | effective |
| effondrement (m) | slump |

| | |
|---|---|
| s'efforcer | to do one's best |
| également | equally |
| égarement (m) | error |
| embouteillage (m) | traffic hold-up |
| émission (f) | broadcast |
| emploi (m) | job |
| emporter sur | surpass |
| en plus | besides |
| endocriniologue-diabétologue (m/f) | specialist in glandular and diabetic disorders |
| énigme (f) | enigma |
| enquête (f) | inquiry |
| enracinement (m) | taking root |
| enseignant (m) | teacher |
| enseignement (m) | teaching |
| entamer | to institute |
| enterrer | to bury |
| entraînement (m) | training |
| entreprise (f) | business |
| environnement (m) | environment |
| épi (m) | ear of corn |
| épreuve (f) | test |
| errance (f) | ramble |
| essaimer | to swarm |
| esthétique | aesthetic |
| estivant (m) | summer holiday maker |
| estrade (f) | platform |
| étain (m) | pewter |
| étendue (f) | stretch |
| étiquette (f) | label |
| éviter | to avoid |
| évoquer | to evoke |
| exclure | to exclude |
| exemplaire (m) | copy |
| exposition (f) | exhibition |

## F

| | |
|---|---|
| (sans) faille | fault (less) |
| faire de la peine | to hurt |
| faire ranger | to line up |
| farder | to make up |
| faux campeurs (m pl) | false campers (*here refugees*) |
| féliciter | to congratulate |
| ferment (m) | yeast |
| (au) fil de l'eau | with the stream |

| | |
|---|---|
| filial | subsidiary |
| fleuronner | to newly blossom |
| floraison (f) | blossoming |
| fondre | to melt |
| force (f) | strength |
| forfaitaire | inclusive |
| formation supérieure (f) | higher education |
| frais d'appel (m pl) | call charges |
| fret (m) | freight |
| frisquet | chilly |
| fuite (f) | flight (*escape*) |

**G**

| | |
|---|---|
| gare à | beware |
| gérer | to manage |
| gestion des stocks (f) | stock control |
| glace polaire (f) | polar ice |
| grandes surfaces (f pl) | large stores |
| grisé | intoxicated |
| groupe de pression (m) | pressure group |
| guerrier | warlike |

**H**

| | |
|---|---|
| haine (f) | hatred |
| harasser | to wear out |
| hebdomadaire | weekly |
| homme d'affaires (m) | business man |
| houle (f) | swell |
| hypertension (f) | hypertension |
| hypothèse (f) | hypothesis |

**I**

| | |
|---|---|
| ignorer | to be unaware of |
| inonder | to flood |
| s'inscrire | to enrol |
| investissement (m) | investment |

**J**

| | |
|---|---|
| jaillir | to gush |
| joyau (m) | jewel |

**L**

| | |
|---|---|
| lâcher | to give up |

| | |
|---|---|
| lancement (m) | launch |
| latte (f) | slat |
| léguer | to bequeath |
| lettre manuscrite (f) | handwritten letter |
| liens (m pl) | bonds |
| lier | to connect |
| lieue (f) | league |
| limbes (f pl) | limbo |
| littoral (m) | shore line |
| lotir | to apportion |

## M

| | |
|---|---|
| main-d'oeuvre (f) | work force |
| maîtriser | to master |
| majoration (f) | increase (*above the norm*) |
| malgré | in spite of |
| maquis (m) | scrub |
| marais salant (m) | salt marsh |
| marastre (OF) | cruel |
| masque de fer (m) | iron mask |
| matière (f) | subject |
| maussade | sullen |
| médecin généraliste (m) | doctor (*general practitioner*) |
| médicament (m) | medicine |
| métamorphose (f) | transformation |
| mignardement | daintily |
| mignonne (f) | darling |
| milliard (m) | one thousand million |
| mise au point (f) | setting up |
| missel (m) | missal |
| mondial | world wide |
| mosquée (f) | mosque |
| mousse (f) | froth, bubbles |
| moût (m) | unfermented wine |
| moyenne (f) | average |
| murer | to wall in |

## N

| | |
|---|---|
| navette (f) | shuttle |
| négrier (m) | slave trader |
| niveau (m) | level |
| nutritioniste (m/f) | nutritionist |

## O

| | |
|---|---|
| occupé | engaged |
| octogénaire (m/f) | octogenarian |
| oeuvre (f) | work |
| ordinateur (m) | computer |
| (d') ores et déjà | from now on |
| outre | in addition to |

## P

| | |
|---|---|
| Président Directeur Général (PDG) | managing director |
| palais de congrès (m) | conference centre |
| parcourir | to travel |
| particulier | private |
| patrimoine (f) | inheritance |
| peau (f) | skin |
| percevoir (pp perçu) | to perceive |
| pierreries (f pl) | precious stones |
| planification (f) | planning |
| pli (m) | fold |
| plumes de poule (f) | hen feathers |
| poignardé | stabbed |
| politique (m/f) | politician |
| poste (m) | extension |
| pourpré | crimson |
| pouvoir (m) | power |
| prendre en charge | to take in hand |
| prendre en compte | to take into account |
| preuve (f) | proof |
| prévoir (pp prévu) | forecast |
| primer | to prime |
| se produire | to happen |
| (au) profit de | for the benefit of |
| pruneau (m) | prune |
| puissance (f) | power |
| puits (m) | shaft |

## Q

| | |
|---|---|
| quartier (m) | district |
| quasi-totalité | almost all |
| ne quittez pas | hold the line (*telephone*) |

## R

| | |
|---|---|
| radio (m) | radio operator |

| | |
|---|---|
| rafale (f) | squall |
| ramage (m) | song (*of birds*) |
| rattrapage (m) | catching up |
| rayonnant | radiant |
| réaliser | to carry out |
| réchauffement (m) | heating |
| rédiger | to draw up |
| redoubtable | to be feared |
| régime (m) | diet |
| réjouissance (f) | merry making |
| remous (m) | eddy |
| renseignements (m pl) | information |
| repère (m) | guide mark |
| réseau (m) | network |
| retentissement (m) | repercussion |
| retraite (f) | retirement, pension |
| roseaux (m pl) | reeds |
| rouille (f) | rust |

## S

| | |
|---|---|
| sagesse (f) | wisdom |
| salorge (f) | salt deposit |
| sangler | to deal |
| sanglier (m) | wild boar |
| sein (m) | bosom |
| self (m) | self-service restaurant |
| seuil (m) | threshold |
| SIDA | AIDS |
| siège centre (m) | head office |
| société (f) | company |
| soufflet (m) | blow |
| soutien (m) | support |
| stage (m) | course |
| suite à | following |
| surhomme (m) | superman |
| surpoids (m) | overweight |
| survie (f) | survival |
| susciter | to give rise to |
| syndiqué (m) | member of a trade union |

## T

| | |
|---|---|
| tarif (m) | fare |
| tâter | to taste |
| taux (m) | amount |
| teint (m) | colour |

| | |
|---|---|
| ternir | to fade |
| tiers monde (m) | third world |
| titulaire (m/f) | holder |
| tortiller | to wriggle |
| tourbe (f) | peat |
| tourbillon (m) | whirlwind |
| tourelle (f) | turret |
| tournesol (m) | sunflower |
| trait d'union (m) | hyphen |
| trajet (m) | journey |
| transmanche | cross channel |
| travailleur (m) | worker |
| tricher | to cheat |
| trombe d'eau (f) | water spout |
| trottant menu | toddling along |
| trou (m) | hole |
| tuyau (m) | pipe |

## U
| | |
|---|---|
| utilisation (f) | use |

## V
| | |
|---|---|
| vague (f) | wave |
| valable | valid |
| vanté | praised |
| véhicule de fonction | company car |
| vendange (f) | grape harvest |
| vesprée (OF) (f) | evening |
| vieillir | to grow old |
| voire | even |

## Y
| | |
|---|---|
| y compris | included |